RAND MERCHANT BANK

We invite you to travel the road
with Obie and to embrace
the magic and madness that is Africa

Obie Oberholzer books supported by Rand Merchant Bank:

Ariesfontein to Zuurfontein – 1988
Southern Circle – 1989
To Hell 'n Gone – 1991
Beyond Bagamoyo – 1996
Raconteur Road – 2000

RaconteurRoad

Road through the Namib Desert. Near Terrace Bay. Skeleton Coast Park. Namibia. '97.

RaconteurRoad

Obie Oberholzer

SHOTS INTO AFRICA

David Philip • Cape Town

Image supplied by Tony Meintjes Photography Studio • 6 Beach Road, Old Castle Breweries Building, Woodstock

The dust road stretches in travellers eye. The road is elongated triangle of vibra (167)

The author thanks:
- Rand Merchant Bank
- Agfa for sponsoring all my photographic materials
- Teltron for giving me a new 6x7 Pentax II camera body plus metering prism and a 135mm Macro lens
- Rhodes University
- Lynn, Nikki and Jesse for their love and support

Technical information
6x7 Pentax camera bodies, with Pentax 35mm, 45mm, 55mm, 135mm Macro, 200mm, 300mm and 500mm lenses. CT Metz electronic flashes, Coleman 1 million Candela torch, Minolta V Flashmeter and Manfrotta tripod.
All photographs were taken on Agfa Optima 120 colour negative roll film and printed on Agfacolor Signum CN 310 glossy paper using Super Chromega and Beseler colour enlargers and developed in the Agfa PRO Colour Processor using Agfa Process 94 Professional colour chemistry.

First published 2000 by David Philip Publishers, 208 Werdmuller Centre, Newry Street, Claremont, 7708

ISBN 0-86486-368-3

Design and layout by *Abdul Amien*
Reproduction by *Scan Shop, Cape Town*
Printed by *ABC Press, Epping, South Africa*

from twenty barmen
maasai under acacias
big game hunters
over terrible potholes
to hemingway's viglia

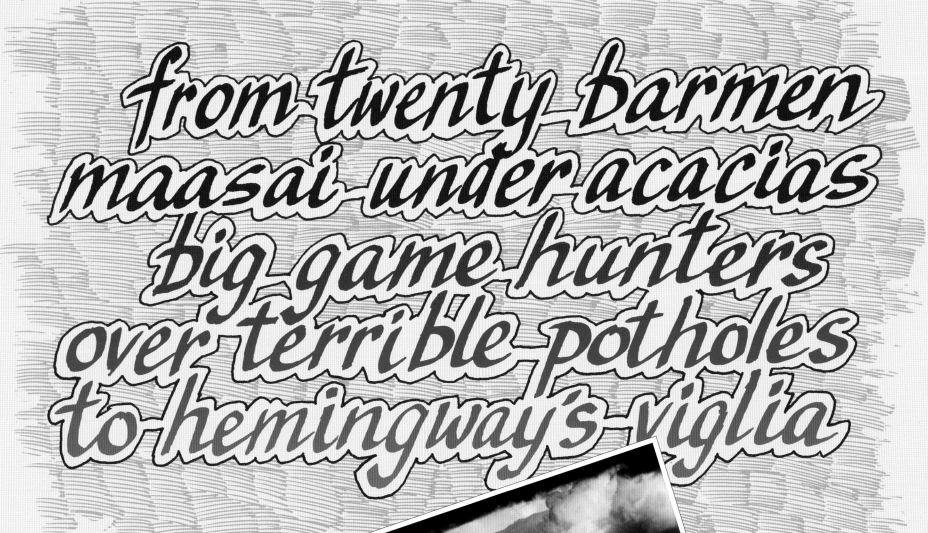

Mr. R. Rohner. Hotel swimming pool.

Kenyan coastline north of Mombasa. '99.

Hemingway's Viglia. Kilimanjaro Buffalo Lodge. Southern Kenya. '99.

The 4x4 lunged and lurched forward at the pace of a dung beetle. I looked across at my companion, the *Stern* magazine writer Peter Sandmeyer, and gave him a tough, savannah grimace. The potholed track made our bodies jostle and sway in synchronised movements. We had left the humid Kenyan coastline early and were crawling our way inland, following the hunting safari trails of the legendary writer Ernest Hemingway. He asked me what a dung beetle looked like. Some way on, I stopped at antelope dung droppings on the road and showed him a small black beetle pushing a huge ball of dung backwards. It took a massive amount of effort and concentration for the small insect to push a large amount of shit forwards. He leant forwards, peering down at the scene in amazement, and said, 'Ach, du liebe Gott, es ist ja unglaublich!' I gently put my finger on the ball of dung, which immediately made the beetle change to low-range 6-wheel drive to get more traction. Slowly, it moved from my grip to continue its journey. I stared at the bit of green dung left on my finger and said, 'We are just like that beetle: it tries to move a large amount of shit forwards but facing backwards, and we try to move forwards to get a whole amount of crap behind us.' A group of Maasai warriors had gathered and were watching these two funny white people, sitting on their haunches in the middle of nowhere, looking at dung droppings. Once out of Tsavo West National Park we headed to the village of Oliotokitok, which lies near the Tanzanian border and the snowclad colossus of Kilimanjaro. We passed a group of giraffes stretching their necks to feed on the flat canopies of acacia thorns. Later that afternoon, I suddenly noticed that our two heads weren't jerking along in synchronisation, which meant that we were losing air in one tyre. With dung beetle courage, and savannah luck, we finally managed to crawl into the Kilimanjaro Buffalo Lodge. To our complete surprise, we found that Hemingway had camped here in December 1953. Towards evening, David Mabwa brought us drinks around a fire as we listened to the hyenas bark under a wide twilit sky.

3

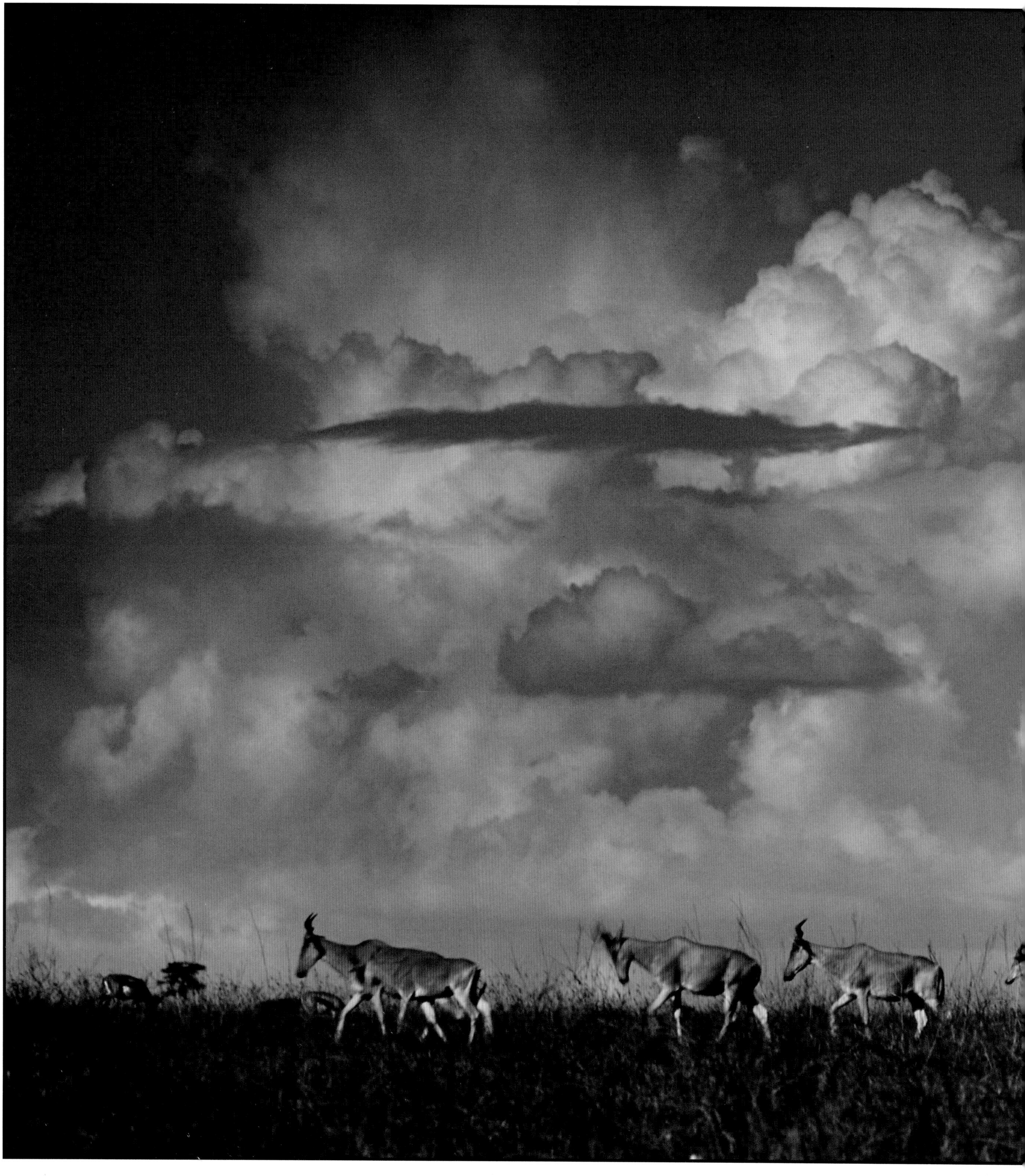

Tsavo West National Park. Southern Kenya. '99.

Safaris Unlimited hunting tent. Southern Kenya. '99.

From a historical perspective, photography has always been at its most comfortable documenting the present, and less so in the representation of the future or the past. With the introduction of all forms of computer-enhanced images, scenes of the past and especially futuristic impressions are easily obtainable. The fact remains that a camera records only what it sees, at a specific moment in time. It is a document written in tonal values of black and white or areas of colour combinations, hue and saturation. If the objects in front of the camera are absorbing, strange, beautiful, sad, happy, the result should be a two-dimensional representation of the original scene. I don't believe that one photograph is better than another; rather, one is more interesting than another. So, basically, 'you get what you take'. If the objects in front of the camera are interesting enough, you 'take them', and if they are not, then you have to 'make them'. Any scene that shifts away from the present and engages the hereafter or the past must first be designed and constructed, and only then photographed. Most hunters and historians will agree that the best and often biggest African hunting safaris took place during the earlier part of the twentieth century. As I am neither hunter nor historian, my job is simply to make 1999 look like 1935, by finding and moving objects into interesting positions in front of the camera. That's the easy part. More difficult is to conjure up a moment in the distant past when Sir Philip Percival peers out of his tent at the darkening bush and the firelight. Then he walks out and sits down next to his hunting partner, Francis Macomber. Peace descends on them as they both have a long drink of bourbon. Philip turns and says, 'God dammit, Francis, that great buffalo almost charged me straight to heaven!' Francis looks at him with a smile. 'You mean straight to hell, ol' pal, it dropped down dead two metres in front of you. Cheers!'

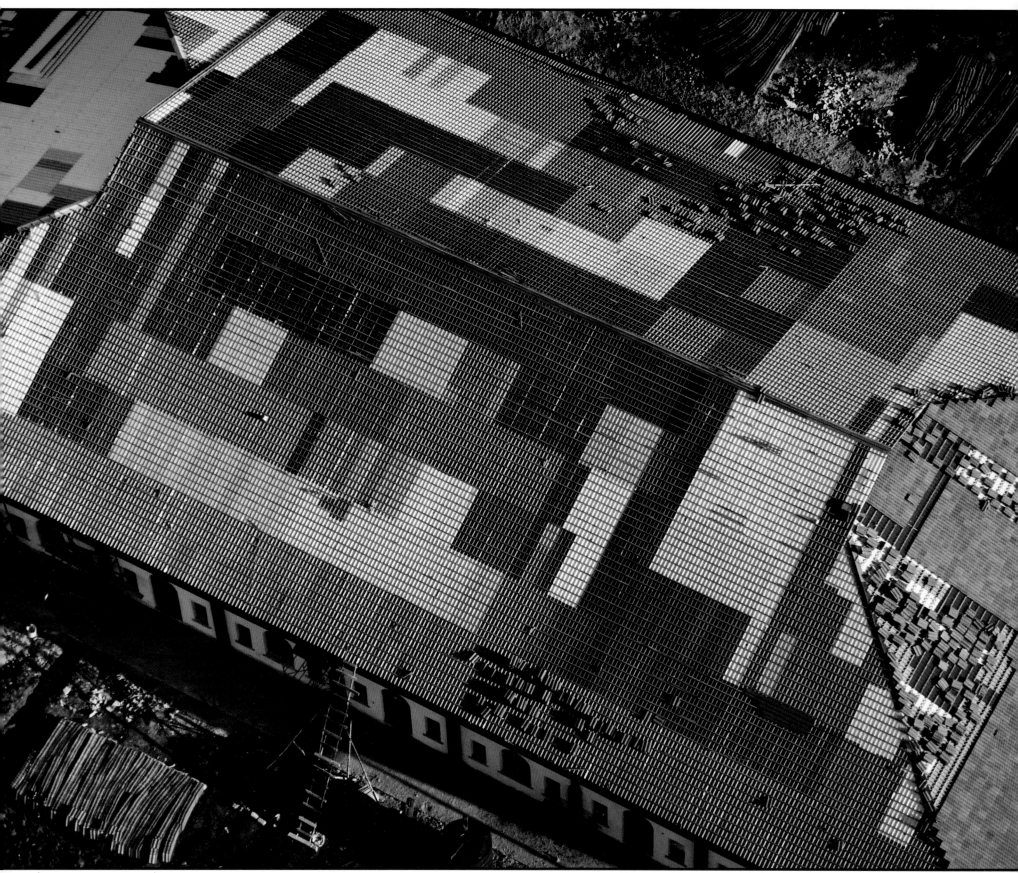

Roof under construction. Outskirts of Nairobi. '99.

Maasai youths. Between Cloitokitok and Ol Tukai. Southern Kenya. '99.

For centuries, the Maasai have lived on the great savannah plains that stretch south of the Great Rift Valley; east, west and north of that big old mountain that often stands with his head of white hair in the clouds. They herded their cattle to places where the cumulus clouds brought green to the parched land. The men were brave warriors who fought the Taita, the Kamba, the Kipsigis and the Embu with their long spears. It became their land, their mountain, all that lay beneath their wide sky. Then slowly, as the years rolled on, came the scouts, pioneers, hunters, missionaries, traders and columns of soldiers. The Maasai stood in little groups, leaning on their spears, beneath the shade of flat-topped acacia trees. Great white hunters came and passed them by with wagons and an entourage of dark-skinned bearers. Some would stop and show them how a long metal thing could kill a buck in the distance with only a bang and a puff of smoke. Others came and told them they now lived in a place called 'Kenya' and that they shouldn't trek across the plains to a place now called 'Tanzania'. That is after the Germans and the British had fought each other with those long pipes that blow smoke and kill. Many years later, they watched as Land Rovers and buses came, full of people who pointed black boxes at them that went 'click' and didn't smoke and kill. They realised, with the years, that these people would give them money to point their boxes. As the tourists increased and their boxes got smaller and fancier, they could ask for more money. The cars became bigger and better, the people inside them richer. They gave them more and more money as long as they could point their cameras to show other rich people at home how the Maasai have lived unchanged for centuries on the savannahs of Africa.

We all know what makes Africa Africa. It is its beauty, its vastness, its mystery, its grandeur and its spirit of adventure. Another point to add to the long list is – its unpredictability. Although I am a pale male in the true African sense, I'll always be with her and she with me. Her rivers flow through my veins, her plains stretch into my heart, and her mountains fold into my mind. She makes me what I am. Visitors of Africa often ask, 'Why?' 'Why this? Why that?' I try to explain that because Africa is so unpredictable, inexplicable and strange, the less you ask 'why?' the easier you'll get along. I was driving with my newly arrived German friend through southern Kenya between Kimana and Makutano. The road was beyond shit. Firstly, I taught him to say 'Scheisse', not in a short, staccato, Germanic way, but in a more passionate, elongated and gentle brutal way. We practised together, from pothole to donga. Once I stopped the 4x4, got out and shouted, 'Thank you, Lord, thank you!' When we were going again, he asked, 'Why did you do that?' 'Because,' I replied, 'I had to stop and thank someone for getting into third gear, once.' Near Makutano, I stopped and pointed my camera at three rocks in an empty landscape. Peter asked, 'Why are you pointing your camera at three rocks?' I motioned at the desolate landscape, 'In Africa, if you think you're alone, beware: you're probably not.' After ten minutes, three Maasai women walked from over the horizon, sat on the rocks, asked for money, and motioned that they were now ready to be photographed.

The anti-malaria drug Larium makes me dream. As I am a rather shallow, happy-go-lucky kind of guy, all my dreams are sweet and pleasant. The real-life nightmares in Africa happen elsewhere. I had dreamt that I was a hero, an author, a hard drinker, a lover and, on top of all that, a famous great white hunter. I sat in front of a large fire with a double whisky nestled in my strong hands. A large group of beautiful girls from a nearby village were dancing topless near the fire; the curves of their bodies moved and glistened in the glow. This was paradise – the power and looks of a hero, sex, booze and, surrounding this, the African bush full of thousands of animals to shoot. The bright sunrise of the following morning brought with it a deep and terrible urge within me. It wasn't an urge to fondle glistening young bodies, nor to shoot a charging lion between the eyes, nor to order a wake-up gin and tonic. I had an urge to become visually erect, find and photograph two great white hunters in Kenya. I thought of some of my rich and powerful friends, who were also some of the last of the great white hunters. They would have been terribly proud of me, standing in the early African light, so visually erect. Towards evening, I managed to track down Tony and Gordon Church, two great white hunters. After having satisfied my visual urge, I asked them about the analogies between big game hunting, masculinity and sexual performance. Slightly aloof, they glanced at each other and chuckled. Tony, the father, said, 'Well, whatever you do – enjoy it and take your time, shoot straight, and never drink and shoot.'

Along the Indian Ocean coastline of Kenya, there's a bar named after Hemingway. The place is decorated with giant stuffed fish, animal trophies, hunting artefacts and photographs of Hemingway in various macho poses – standing next to a massive marlin, with dead kudus, rhinos and buffaloes. The bar counter has a large circular shape made of oak, supporting a trellis from which hangs a large assortment of beer mugs. Behind me, there was a more pensive portrait of Hemingway, sitting on a boat between fishing rods. I can't remember what I was drinking, but it must have been a lot, if one counted the circular stains left on the counter. I smiled at the tall blonde German next to me, because she had big broad lips and large tits. A long day in Africa had put me into one of those bullshitty moods. I stood up, peered through one of the beer mugs with the circular indentations, and looked at the barman, who wore a red fez and a bright floral shirt that seemed like psychedelic seaweed. The glass refracted the scene into a multitude of images, making at least twenty smiling barmen. This was great and made me roar with laughter. The German girl was enthralled by all this and asked if she could also look through the beer mug. I said that it would be visually much more intoxicating if she did it naked. This made her giggle. I quickly had to check if old Ernest was still brooding between his fishing rods. After the German girl had seen the twenty smiling barmen through the beer glass, she broke out in a sexy chuckle. This made me wish I had a rod like Ernest. She asked me what I did. I pushed the Jeffrey Meyers biography of Hemingway towards her and said, 'I am a photographer following his footsteps. Open page 426, third paragraph.' She found the page and read, 'Hemingway had announced that spilling sperm no longer interfered with spilling ink. Of his 50th birthday, he wrote ... I fucked three times, shot ten straight at pigeons at the club, drank with five friends a case of Piper Heidsieck Brut, and looked at the ocean of big fish all afternoon.' The barman roared with laughter at least twenty times and the German girl lost her sexy chuckle.

Hemingsways Hotel Bar. Southern Kenyan coastline. '99.

Hemingways Hotel. Near Malindi. Southern Kenyan coastline. '99.

Soon after landing in Mombasa, I quickly surrendered myself to the chaotic and completely mad bustle of this coastal city. On the plane, I had finished reading Ernest Hemingway's *Green Hills of Africa*: the book had added an extra gloss to my personification of the rough and tough African raconteur. You need this image when attempting to hire a taxi, otherwise it'll hire you. I walked tall, a little too slow, the one leg dragging slightly with a limp (leg mauled by lion). At intervals, my right arm would ride a couple of paces on my hip (pelvis shattered by charging buffalo). Although my left eye twitched nervously (bush war injury), they were both screwed up and mean (probably from all the years of deep-sea fishing). The road out of Mombasa, north along the coast, is an exhilarating drive through shanties, shops, shit, bars, food stalls, rubbish dumps, and stray dogs. Hemingway's, outside Malindi, is one of those slightly over-voluptuous luxury coastal hotels. The waiters stood around and jumped at everyone's beck and call, their jackets so exotic that they were probably designed by an Italian who'd lived in Hawaii for too long. Most of the tourists looked pale and ill at ease and, like me, played out their own little African charade. In Africa, if you need to achieve something sooner than later, just go out and do it. Wear sandals, not Nikes. I pointed my camera at the fading light, lapping waters and moving fishing boats, plonked down some fishing rods, found someone who came the closest to looking like a 'big-game fisherman–professional hunter–African adventurer–Hemingway'. It turned out to be a tanned Pommy from Plymouth. I bought him a beer, handed him the *Green Hills of Africa* and said, 'Thanks. Please read from here, it's about a great hunter ...' I photographed and he read, '... of how a man should be, brave, gentle, comic, never losing his temper, never bragging, never complaining except in a joke, tolerant, understanding, intelligent, drinking a little too much as a good man should ...'

balls in the rough
at honde valley
chimanimani man
moonrise over baobabs
to a sad white dove

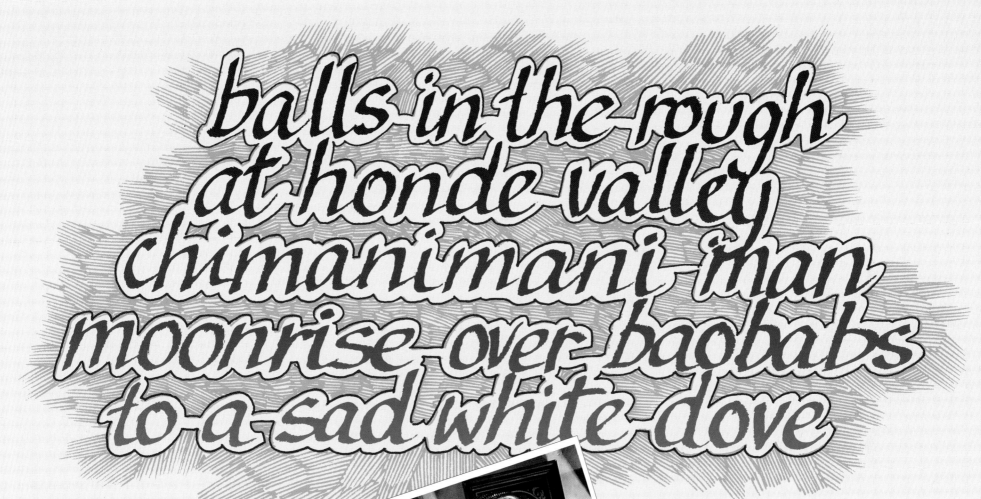

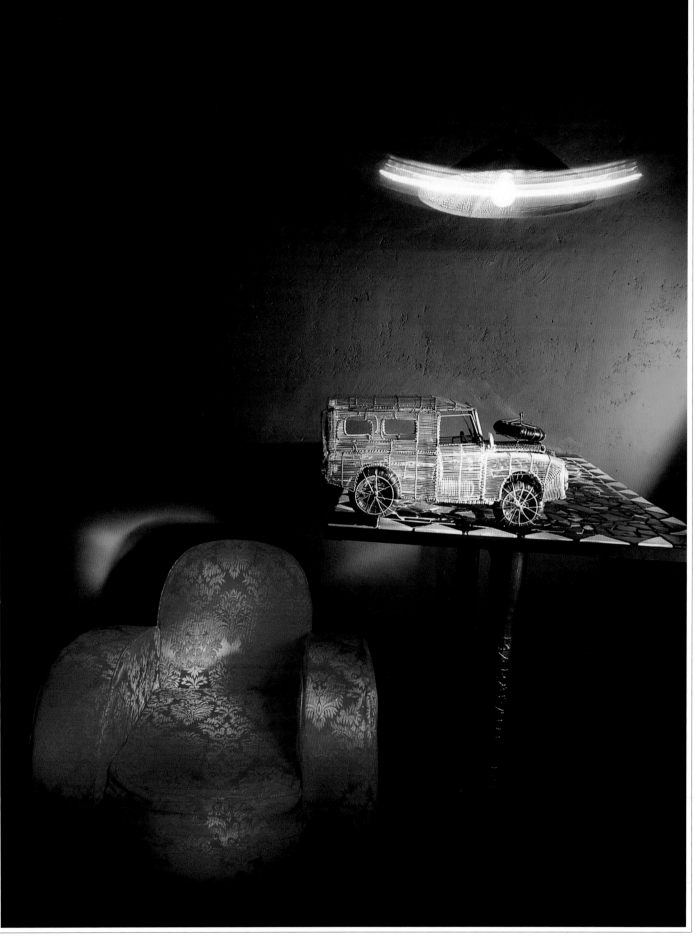

As you drive into the village, the night-club is on your right. If you want to sleep, not jive, go to the hotel; it's across the road, on the left. Behind the bar stood a real pretty girl – Miss Chimanimani, I guessed. I leant on the counter and grinned kind of silly, in a macho way, then glanced around. There was an old Land Rover on the table beneath a lamp, the walls kissed back a thick blue, and the chair oozed voluptuous red. I ordered a Red Rum for my left hand and a passionate blue liqueur for the right one. In Chimanimani, when you mix blue with red, you get purple. The more you mix it, the mauver it gets. My thoughts mauved around, photographic in nature. It's so delicious, mixing pleasure with work. Photo-foreplay is so much nicer than coming straight to the shot. Anyway, what's in a shot of a chair and a wall and a lamp? After an hour of mauving, I'd convinced the bargirl that she was the prettiest girl south of the great Zambezi River, and posing for me would bring her endless pleasure and fame. When I returned with the equipment a few minutes later, she had ... well, honestly, just disappeared, vanished, mauved off. Conclusion in Chimanimani: if you miss it, you miss it.

Nightclub. Chimanimani. Eastern Highlands. Zimbabwe. '99.

Bridal Veil Falls. Chimanimani National Park. Eastern Highlands. Zimbabwe. '99.

Boys and cars. Chimanimani Village. Eastern Highlands. Zimbabwe. '99.

Birchenough Bridge over the Save River. Manicaland. Zimbabwe. '99.

Telephoto lenses isolate sections of a large landscape, usually placing the photographer at a viewpoint that is distant from the scene. Perspective in a scene is the relationship between objects to each other. In this instance, the objects are said to be pushed together or flattened. Perhaps a better word would be compressed. We can all see that the baobab is behind the hut and in front of the bridge, but by standing far away we now 'feel' that the three objects are pushed together and are interacting with each other. This is the easy part, which any photographic student learns in Grade 1. What the hell was I doing here anyway, in the middle of the bush, pointing a camera at a baobab and a bridge? Compositionally the picture was bad, too. It needed something (a white sheet on the washing line) on the left to balance the confusing lines on the right. I wanted to walk the 150 metres and ask the dude in the white shirt for a white sheet, but I couldn't because I was scared some local might want to take up a new career in photography and so flatten my perspective completely. Shouting these compositional requests over that distance would've been more difficult than going to Mars. That was that and here's a lopsided picture of a house, a baobab and a bridge.

19

It was one of those hot, dry African days, where the drought goes up your nose and lazes around your brain. After the engine had died, the shrill cries of the cicadas picked up again, like an endless orchestra of violins playing at their shrillest. Frank leant on the wire and I, slightly bent, had my hands on my hips. We faced each other, tense and ready, like long ago in Tombstone at the OK Corral. He fired, I fired, boom-boom, and the orchestra died. Frank blew the smoke from his fingers, smiled and said, 'Hey, big Mazungu [white man], it's very bright, you would shoot better if you bought a hat'. I walked up to him, looked down and smiled, 'OK, black man, why are you standing here like a cowboy, shooting your mouth off?' The cicada chorus came alive. Frank pointed left and then right. 'You, rich Mazungu, you buy mat for your one wife and broom for the other'. I pointed at him: 'And you, little black man, go back to school'. Frank pushed his hat back, pointed at the hanging cloths and read: 'All creatures great and small, all things wise and wonderful, all things bright and beautiful, the Lord God made them all'. Whiteman waved and Blackman grinned. 'You come again, Mazungu, then we shoot some more one day'.

Boy and shop. Near Chipangayi. Manicaland. Zimbabwe. '99.

John holding white dove. Vumba Mountains. Eastern Highlands. Zimbabwe. '99.

It was damn awful when the pompous colonialists were still here in Africa, strutting around with their fake righteousness and foreign philosophies. Once they had left and everyone was free, the shit really hit the fan, and it sprayed all over the continent. The Congolese fought each other, and died; the Biafrans fought and starved, and died even more; Christian minorities fought Islamic majorities; Hutus murdered Tutsis; Eritreans lay dead next to Ethiopians; and Idi Amin killed thousands just for kicks. The 'goodies' chopped up the 'baddies', the 'baddies' disappeared in the bush to return later and string up the 'goodies'. The 'baddies' looked like 'goodies', so nobody really knew what the hell was going on. Except the United Nations, of course, who knew everything but did nothing. General This would oust General That, who promised everyone bananas, but then ruled till they rotted. The MPLAs chased the UNITAs, the Frelimos ambushed the Renamos, and the Somalian warlords shot up everyone around. Don't cry for Argentina, just weep for Africa and hope and pray that one day the white dove will fly.

Africa is so huge – so dark before it gets light, so vast and bright before the night. After John had put the white dove back in its cage, I drove away, up into the hills. In Africa, it sometimes helps a little to laugh when you cry and to be happy when you're sad. Be orderly in your head and haphazard in your heart. Become sober in your mind and drunk in your soul. Haphazardland. I stopped and looked at a sign, forgotten and old. I think it read, 'Keep well off the road ... [something ... something] long trucks turning'. Look normal and see strange. I found an owl and a bird of prey, a dog and a beast scratching its nose against a pole. There was a crow playing ball, and somewhere a white dove ... flying.

Old road sign near Chimanimani. Manicaland province. Eastern Highlands. Zimbabwe. '99.

Moonrise over baobabs and village near the Devure River bridge. Manicaland Province. Zimbabwe. '99.

I didn't have any Nikes, so I couldn't 'just do it'. At the Devure River bridge a group of young boys were just hanging around. They looked fine and I felt fine. There were potholes on the road, cracks in the bridge and baobabs in the bush. It's difficult executing a plan when everything's so fine. Then one boy came forward, leant on my window and said, 'I am hungry, give me money'. His name was Lovemore. In Africa, most plans only start to happen when things are not all that fine. 'Lovemore!' I said. 'Lovemore! I like that. I'll give you money, if you show me baobabs, a village with huts and a moon'. Then we drove off the road, across the veld, Lovemore in the front and the other boys in the back. We drove through villages where people just stared, along footpaths and cattle tracks. Sometimes, Lovemore would jump off and run in front, rolling away rocks, pulling away branches and moving obstacles that you find in the African bush. How weird it must have looked, a dirty grey-green 1985 Toyota Corolla, packed with boys and Lovemore on the bonnet directing the way. Later, the boys made a fire, baobabs stood, the camera exposed (±2 hours), the moon rose. Lovemore got his money and all around the bush everything was quiet and fine again.

Tea plantations and huts. Honde Valley, Eastern Highlands. Zimbabwe. 99,

Emmanuel Chikwe was a real cool dude. He lived in a small house without a number, but his address was PO Box 92, Chimanimani. The mist was cool, hanging about the village in the early morning. I was from Box 94 in the City of Saints and also trying to act cool. This was more an outward cool than an inward one, mainly 'cause my body got too fired up on all the Red Rum the previous night. It was real cool, because Emmanuel and I liked each other, and we had lots of time to talk. This was because he had no petrol and I had nowhere to go. Two little children came down the road and I bought them each a cold pie. Emmanuel got nothing, because he had nothing. We talked on, about life, he on his chair and me in the car. We talked about the cool weather, his girls, his loves. How was his wonderful president, Comrade Mugabe? Emmanuel lost his smile. The question wasn't cool. Emmanuel got up and checked my oil, smiled, and said that everything was cool. I checked my watch, then walked to the bottlestore. So there we were, Emmanuel and I, each with a long, cool beer.

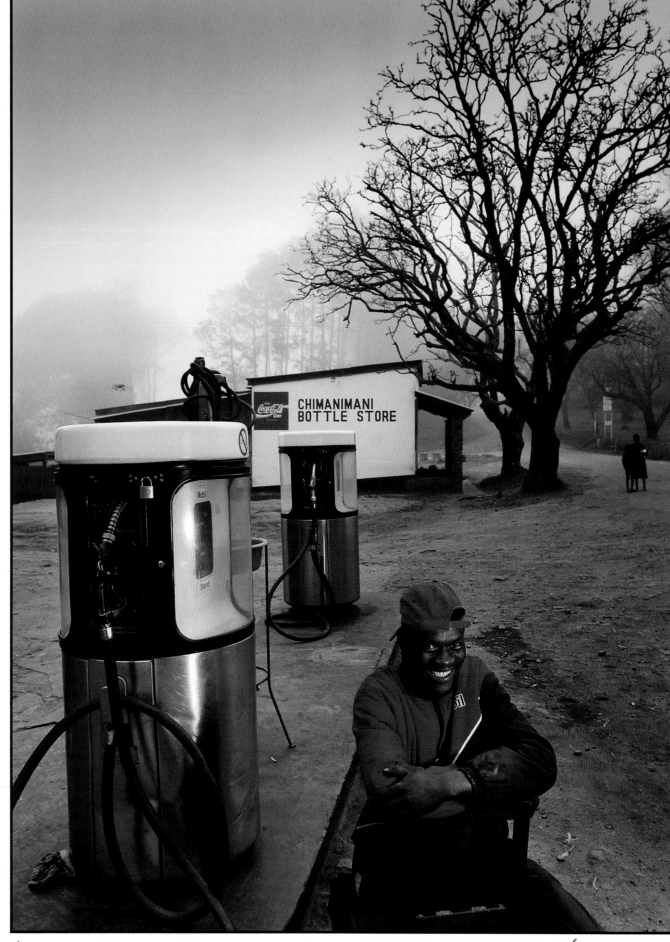

Emmanuel Chikwe. Chimanimani. Eastern Highlands. Zimbabwe. '99.

Restaurant car park. Mamari Lodge. Near the Devure River bridge. Manicaland. Zimbabwe. '99.

Here the jungles of the Vumba mountains tumble down from massive rock cliffs. Creepers turn and wind their way upwards. Giant fig trees droop down their branches, dwarfing one and all. This green flow is stopped by the swooping shapes of the windows of the hotel's entrance hall. Too many waiters scurried around too few tourists. I set up my camera in a corner, flush against a mirror, a brightly lit chandelier placed slap-bang in the middle. It would still be a while before the sun reached its apex, reflecting itself in the mirror. Nobody bothered me, so I wandered off in African thought. It always came to the same – more questions than answers, especially in places as luxurious as this one. A golf course, a sauna, a casino and so much to eat. Not far from here, poverty on arid land. A president who speeds through the land with a cavalcade of black Mercedes-Benzes, tinted windows, bodyguards. Why doesn't he ever stop and look? The sun shone double. Then the lights went out. 'Why now?' I said angrily out loud. I told a waiter, who couldn't hear, 'In Africa, if you think you know, beware: you probably don't.'

Leopard Rock Hotel entrance hall. The Vumba mountains. Eastern Highlands, Zimbabwe. 93.

The Aberfoyle Tea Estates lie right down at the end of the Honde Valley, almost against the Mozambique border. The country club is still surrounded by overgrown concrete bunkers, built by the Rhodesians against Zanu freedom fighters who infiltrated the country from the east. The valley is mountainous and lush and the cultivated tea plantations roll up and down, hugging the hills like a bright green quilt. The local people are some of the friendliest I have ever met in Africa. The golf course twists and turns its way through the natural forest, avenues of eucalyptus trees and tea. I hired clubs and played a round of golf, starting off like a tiger and ending like a warthog. At times I would meet a group of young girls watering the greens. In fact, we seemed to be moving along the course at the same pace, because I spent much time crawling around in the rough, grunting like a warthog looking for food. Often the girls would come and help me look for my balls. Balls? Yes, because I cheat at golf. If my first drive is in the rough, then I try another one. This would often give me two balls in the rough. They would giggle and laugh at me crawling around like a pig. If a golfer can't take being laughed at, don't 'tea' off at Aberfoyle.

Security guards. Aberfoyle Tea Estates. Honde Valley. Eastern Highlands. Zimbabwe. '99.

'Lovemore' washing. Punch Rock guest farm. Nyanga area. Eastern Highlands. Zimbabwe. '99.

In the '30s, the technical aspects of cameras improved so dramatically that the flow of life could be stopped, frozen in sections of split-second time. These frozen moments brought forth images that amazed and often startled a generation. Photographers spoke of this special moment, a moment that came intuitively – 'To know before seeing and to see before knowing.' It was strange that I would be thinking of all this, especially as I was never good at this way of photographing. I prefer to make than to take. To illustrate: The water of the pretty falls gushes gently over the edge, gurgles in the rock pools and ripples away down the stream. Lovely, but not enough. The next step to improve the picture is to get an assistant. This is done by flashing a dollar bill. You now have a large group of over-enthusiastic assistants. To cut down on the number of faces, you flash a five rand coin. You are then left with a tall boy and a fat boy. At this stage, the fact that you are using young people flickers past your eyes. This quickly goes away when you shut them for a second. To make the fat boy thinner, you ask him to run to his village and bring back the prettiest girl. You can visualise it – the water gushing over her beautiful body. He brings back 37-year-old Diana Manyau. She undresses, the water gurgles. You sigh and she laughs. 'To know before seeing and see before knowing.'

Moonrise over Motel swimming pool. Bubi River. Masvingo Province. Zimbabwe. '99.

My **business brain** is worse than that of a warthog, the bad points outweigh the few good ones, and my character is as crooked as my spine (broken in a motorbike accident in 1980). My intentions started nobly, with the full moon rising over the Bubi River. I would drink Coke after Coke, and then later sell the image to World-Wide Coke. Then, at least, I'd be sober, crooked and rich. The moon rose. I phoned my wife and said that I was drinking Coke. She asked if I was ill. The moon rose. When it reached the 'Don't worry' I had a beer, instead of a Coke. When it went beyond the 'Be happy', I was drinking more beer than Coke. I phoned my millionaire friend and said that I was cutting down on the Coke. He said that he was breathtaken by such groundbreaking news. The moon rose. I liked that: 'groundbreaking, breathtaken'. The moon rose and reached the tree. The waiter took the Cokes and brought more beer. The Castles became Zambezis. I phoned a famous old Springbok rugby captain and asked him where his moon was. He replied that it was up his arse, then put the phone down. The moon rose. The Zambezis changed to Black Labels. I found that really funny: the thought of a moon rising up someone's arse. The waiter had dozed off. The moon rose and reached the top of the tree. Too much Coke is bad for you. 'Be happy, don't worry.'

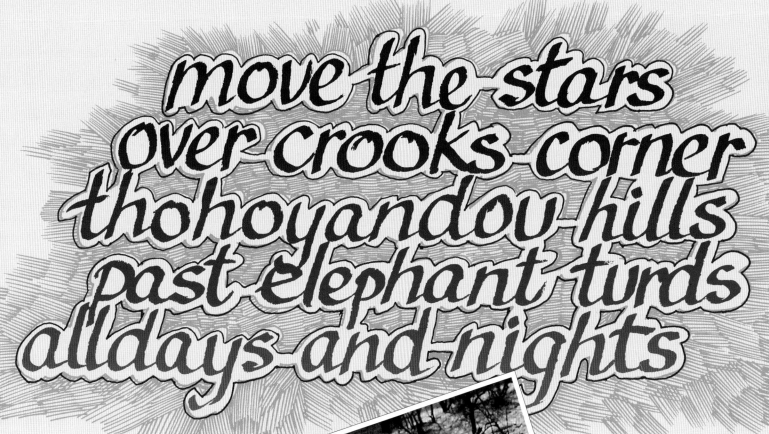

move the stars
over crooks corner
thohoyandou hills
past elephant turds
alldays and nights

Artist Rosina Manaka. Rural area west of Pietersburg. Northern Province. South Africa. '99.

Suzi Zondwani. School girl. Rural area south of Louis Trichardt. Northern Province. South Africa. '99.

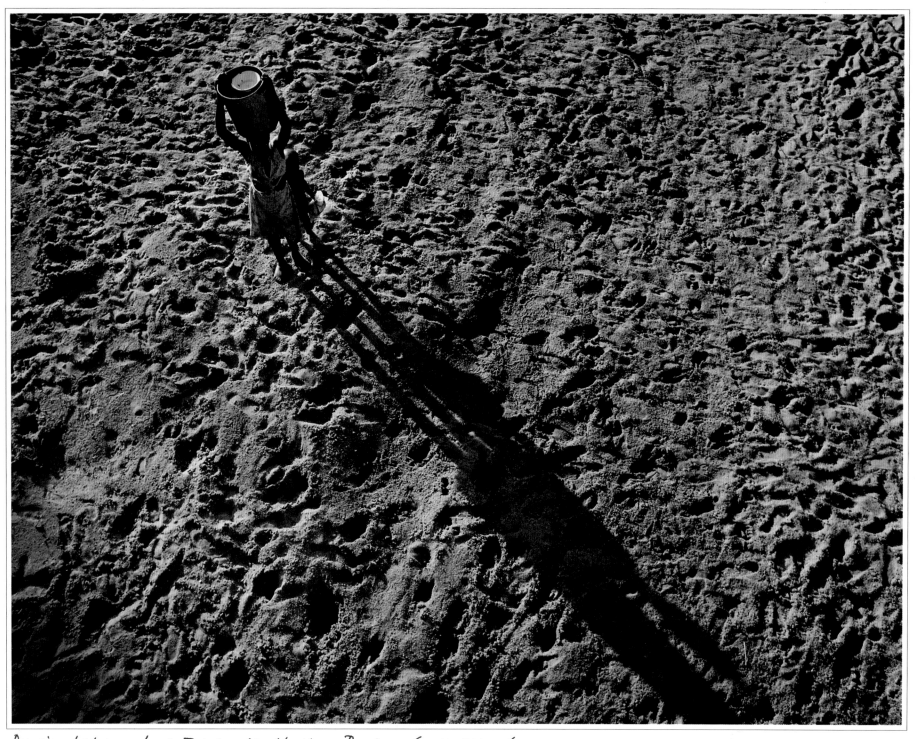

Dry riverbed near Louis Trichardt. Northern Province. South Africa. '99.

Herman Potgieter
27.1.45 – 13.2.98

I could feel the strong downward push of air from the rotary blades above. If I had been born American, I would have felt the same when flying over Vietnam shooting 300 rounds a minute at invisible Vietcong below. Now I looked down at some waterbuck and a herd of buffalo grazing amongst the trees, firing a 67 Pentax at 1/1000 of a second at f5.6. We circled steeply, and chopped at the hot air above South Africa, Zimbabwe and Mozambique. We crossed the confluence of the Luvuvhu and Limpopo rivers. The pilot pointed down and his voice crackled through my earphones: 'Down, nine o'clock, Crooks Corner coming up'. Crooks Corner, I then remembered, was named after the ivory smugglers who around the 1900s used to evade police capture by escaping from one country to another. I thought of my old friend Herman Potgieter, that crazy aerial photographer. It was two years ago that he died, when his plane crashed into the Ngong Hills outside Nairobi. I took the bottle of champagne from my camera case and pushed out the cork – 'Chuck-a-chuck-a-chuck-POP-chuck-a-chuck-a-chuck'. The pilot crackled through my earphones. 'What the hell is going on?' he shouted. 'Alpha-Bravo, picking up enemy ground fire. Circle Crooks Corner again … repeat … circle Crooks Corner!' Then I closed my eyes, said a short prayer and gulped down half the bottle. While we were flying over the river, I threw out the other half and shouted, 'For you, old friend, go well!' The air felt good, and I knew that Herman was around me in the sky, slightly pissed and laughing.

41

Deba Modjagi – 13 year old mother. Tomato farm near Mooketsi. Northern Province. South Africa. '99.

Gardener Jele-Maleleke with Bougainvillea tree. Modjagi area. Northern Province. South Africa. '99.

View near Punda Maria. Madsaringe river course. Kruger National Park. Northern Province. South Africa. '99.

The big bull elephant walked up the road. Now and again, he would stop and eat leaves from the side, then slowly lumber on. He seemed in no giant hurry with this stopping and starting, and eating, and lumbering on. I guessed that passing him wouldn't be such a good idea, and besides there were thousands of photographs of elephants from the front. With his forward lumbering he would also sway sideways. These movements would take up most of the road. As we both had so much time on hand, I opened my pocket dictionary and smiled: this was the first time I had looked up a word driving behind an elephant's behind. 'Lumber', I read aloud, 'to move in blundering, noisy way'. I then named him 'Great Blunder'. After a good while, he stopped rather strangely, then dropped some of the biggest turds I have ever seen. I was so close to him that I could hear them drop. Boom 1, Boom 2, Boom 3, 4, 5 and Boom 6!! Then Great Blunder flapped his ears, swished his tail and lumbered away into the bush. When all was clear, I picked up the biggest turd, wrapped it up and made space for it in the boot of my car. Thus was conceived my bright new business venture, for local and overseas markets – 'The Great African Turd Company'. (They would be non-smelling, varnished, mounted on a stand and individually labelled Blunder 203, Blunder 204, Blunder 205, etc.)

Smaller herds of elephant often cross from the Tuli Block in eastern Botswana and roam the Limpopo floodplain west of Pontdrift. One evening, I could hear them approaching my camp, grunting and feeding, breaking branches from the trees that grow along the riverbed. There was a faint breeze blowing from the west. I left my camera on time exposure and, armed with a portable flash and powerful hunting torch, I slowly crept closer to them, keeping the wind at my back. A somewhat shaky voice had whispered in my ear that 'life without adventure is not life at all'. Soon, I could distinguish about twelve large shapes gently rocking back and forth as they munched and scratched in the dry vegetation. My body screamed at the joy of being so close to the greatness of nature. My heart was pounding in my eyes, and the dust that rose up from beneath their feet smelt pungent and old. The leading bull must have sensed my presence, for he raised his head and looked round. Then, suddenly, he charged out from the dark. I spun round and ran in hasty panic. He stopped, then charged again. I managed to fire off one flash before diving over the single-wire electric fence. I suggest that this technique of photographing elephants should be used with utmost caution.

'Ting' went the microwave and out came the pie. 'Clang' went the till and back came the change. A pudgy hand pushed the goods across the counter. My head was rotten and my tongue rough on that Sunday morning in the Sonskyn Café. I looked down at the scene and counted: five fat fingers with two rings on them, one pie and a Red Bull drink. Then I glanced past the cheap bangles, the bags of wobbly skin under the upper arms, a thin gold chain amongst the folds of her neck. The woman had a round face, broad lips and wrinkles that she had tried to cover up for last night's dance. Round her head, she had tied what looked like a dishcloth and on her left cheek there was a large mole with hair growing out of it. I swallowed slowly, not from hunger, but from a bad thirst. 'Thanks,' I said, pointing at the Red Bull. 'Gives you wings.' I went outside and sat on the pavement, poking at my pie. It was old, very hot on the outside and cold on the inside. Two little happy boys came past on their way to church, smiled and were gone. I wiped my mouth and thought: Sunday morning coming down, with the good, the bad and the ugly.

Two young boys going to church. Louis Trichardt. Northern Province. South Africa. '99.

Raffiek Mushumi is the grandson of Jackson Hlungwani – one of the famous sculptors of Vendaland. Raffiek said that the old man had gone away that day to think about the many matters that lay on the road between earth and heaven. He did not know what these matters were. Often his grandfather would speak in parables. 'After you have carved a sculpture from a block of wood from the marula tree, you must collect all the chips lying around you. They are little voices from the big tree. Then, throw them into the fire and you will see the marula's spirit dance in the smoke.' Raffiek disappeared into his hut. He returned with some small wooden sculptures that he had carved. When he showed me one that was white with a funny face he started to laugh. 'This one, here, looks just like you.' It was made from a piece of the marula tree. I smiled, shook my head and said, 'And I suppose, if you throw it in the fire, I will jump up and dance like the spirits of the marula tree?' Raffiek held the sculpture below his chin. 'No, we will dance from the smoke of another piece. You will buy this one, to keep for the day you will speak about the many matters between heaven and earth, and I will have money to buy some new books for my school.'

Norbert Hahn. Soutpansberg mountains. Northern Province. South Africa. '99.

Finding Norbert Hahn was more difficult than finding King Solomon's mines. He lives alone, north of Louis Trichardt, tucked away in the Soutpansberg. His small house stands next to a stream beneath steep orange cliffs and was filled with artefacts, books, rocks, sculptures, presses, masks, skulls and everything imaginable from the Northern Province. 'Well, Norbert,' I said, 'I am here because people in the district say that you're rather strange, hidden away here in the mountains, researching all kinds of ... of ...' Norbert continued for me, rearranging a buffalo skull: 'I am a self-styled archaeologist, zoologist, botanist, ecologist' – he placed some Venda beads on a metre-high wooden penis – '... anthropologist and environmentalist.' The setting looked just like it had come out of some adventure-movie set of the sixties. 'Have you always been like this?' I asked, arranging the baboon skull in front of the boxes of Agfa-chrome film. 'Since school,' he answered, 'where they branded me everything from a madman to an idiot.'

I know a farmer called George, who lives up north near the Brandboontjierivier [Chillibean River]. His farm is called 'Rolvark'. Literally, this means Rolling Pig, named after the time he had shot a very large wild pig on the top of the *koppie*. It was so big that they had to roll the pig down the hill. Him and his wife, Ramona, are the friendliest and kindest people south of Messina. George's hobby is cultivating orchids. He had them all, from the *Angraecum* to *Zygopetalum*. That afternoon, we started the fire for the braai early, and the conversation was burning well. George spoke about a new orchid he had cultivated, the 'Leopard Orchid'. More people arrived. This stoked George up even more. I fled and joined a subdued lady in the far corner, as far away from the blazing fire, orchids and leopards as possible. I was already sitting when I realised that she wore a leopard blouse. Her name was Engela Elizabeth Helena de Villiers and I said, 'Nice fire'. Then a dark man came running out of the black bush. The fire glistened on the sweat of his body. The whites of his eyes jumped round and round. He said that the Rollvark labourers had captured a thief, an illegal *tsotsi* from Mozambique, whom they had dealt with and tied up in the shed. This added fuel to the fire. It was becoming quite a night amongst the orchids, spotted blouses, leopards and *tsotsis* from Mozambique.

Engela de Villiers

Leopard orchid with Engela de Villiers. Rolvark Farm. Mooketsi area. Northern Province. South Africa. '99.

Suspected thief and illegal immigrant. Roodvaark Farm. Northern Province. South Africa. '99.

The **twin-track** leading to the baobab was better than the main track. The latter connected one village to another and I suppose that's why it was called a main track. Anyway, it was just a long way full of dongas, and potholes, and corrugations, and rocks, and other objects that made for the use of strong language. True Roadism is the ability to swear creatively from village to village, while zigzagging double the distance, to the sound of your car packing up from laughter. Just beyond the one village, I picked up little barefoot Vusi, who was convinced he was going to the other village. It's a little difficult having a conversation between all the laughing, swearing and zigzagging. Through all this Roadism, Vusi was learning fast and I am convinced to this day that he learnt some powerful new adjectives. He also learnt that when a man's got to go, he's got to go, and stop when he's got to stop. Teaching by example brings a great deal of satisfaction, like two boys weeing together against a giant baobab. Before we set off to more cursing and corrugations, I explained to Vusi that all these strong bad things he'd been hearing (and most bad things in life) could be blamed on apartheid. Vusi got in the car again and said, 'We all @$^^!?##! free now, no more ^!%#!!^#!^! apartheid.' We laughed and zigzagged on from the baobab to the next village.

Baobab tree near the village of Tshiungani. Malonga Plains. Northern Province. South Africa. '99.

Across the Soutpansberg, on the Bushveld plains east of Musisodi, stands one of the oldest living things on earth – a giant old baobab. Its giant bulk, the circumference of which counted almost fifty paces, tortured and turned its way skywards. Some branches, higher up, turned back towards the earth below, as if pulled down by their own weight. Its outer contours looked like twisted and compressed columns of lava that had pushed up from the earth's core. This tree had no bark; it had a hide with a metallic copper-grey sheen, gnarled and marked by time. On the western side, perhaps two metres up, a thin opening led the way into the tree's inner chamber. Once inside, it was dim and absolutely quiet, lit only by a small crack somewhere higher up. I thought back to the tree near Mooketsi, where a farmer had built a bar inside a baobab tree. It's really important that everyone should experience life from inside a tree and feel the inner spirit of a giant beast. Last time I could wash my thoughts down with a beer or two but this time I had been swallowed alone. A while later, whilst photographing, I suddenly realised that the shapes around me looked like elephant legs. I wondered again how anyone could believe that I had stood amongst a herd of elephants inside a tree.

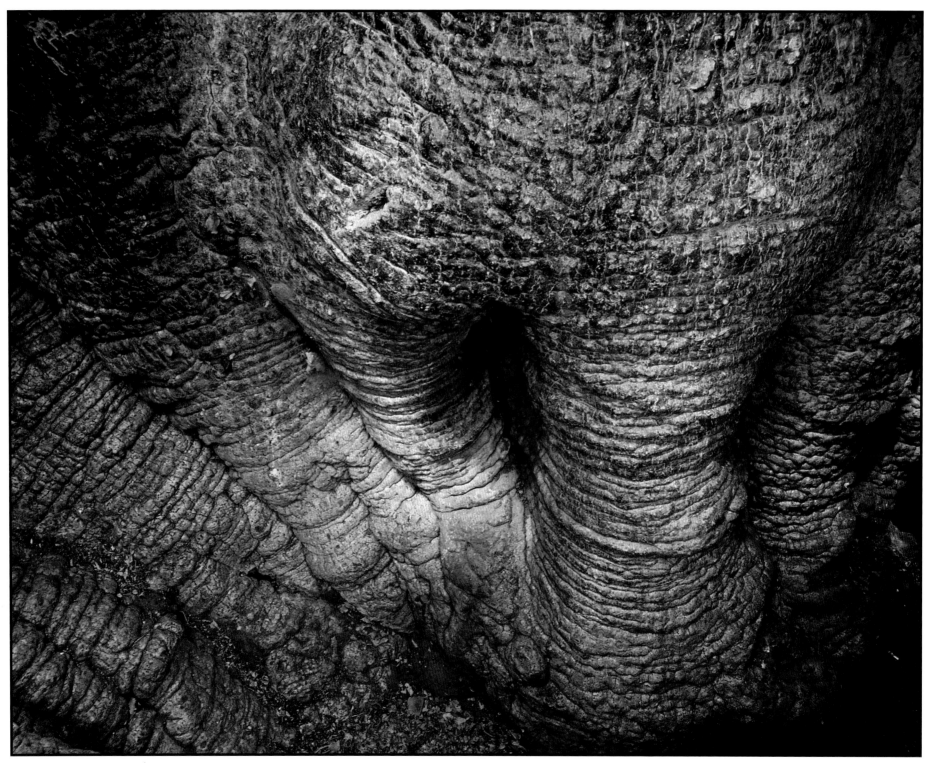

Elephant shapes inside baobab tree. Near Muswodi. Northern Province. South Africa. '99.

55

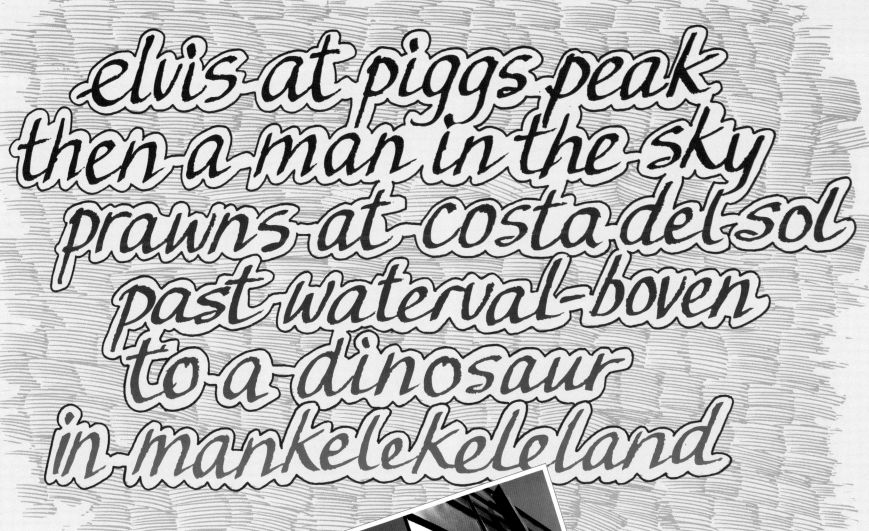

elvis at piggs peak
then a man in the sky
prawns at costa del sol
past waterval-boven
to a dinosaur
in mankelekeleland

Mother and child along the road to Moamba. Southern Mozambique. '99.

So often, the sadness of a scene just gets me and, like a cancer, grows. More is taken than is given. Under a cloak of superficiality, I momentarily record a little section of the large, yet knowing full well that my dark glasses hide the poverty and despair. You drive on, shrugging away questions, all down the road. The road is your crutch, your macho mate, a happy song whose chorus is sad. The serious and the straight become roadfellows along with the trivial and the dishonest. You are a pirate of light, a wayward traveller – happy, yet sad. You argue away the poverty with this, and the despair with that, and at the end of the day, you've missed the potholes because they were there. When the hadedas have flown their goodbyes, you look up from the fire's flames to find the melancholy in the evening sky.

Peggy Walker. Sabie. Mpumalanga. South Africa. '99.

Peggy Walker lifted the glass neatly to her mouth, then sipped the wine with style. I found my own mouth, took a gulp, then wiped my face. I did some visual navigation around the parts of her body which appeared above the table and smiled; the co-ordinates looked healthy and large. She took a fancy napkin and gently patted the drop of red wine remaining at the corner of her mouth. Her bangles gave a little jingle as she placed her finger on her chin and said, 'Don't tell me that you are one of those horny men who gloat around women peering down their cleavages.' 'No, no, no ... no,' I retorted strongly, 'no, definitely not one of those macho male chauvinists.' I filled my glass and tried to sip it gently, with style, but spilt some wine down the front of my shirt. She leant forward with confidence and said, 'Wine stains, you know. What are you then, a leopard with no spots?' I wiped my face again, 'No, no ... no, I am a ... mm ... a visual vagabond.' A couple of months later I phoned her in Dullstroom and said that the photograph I had taken had come out fine except for the fact that her one boob looked much larger than the other. 'Oh,' she answered on the phone (straightfaced I suppose), 'say that I was having a mammogram, and when I pulled away, the one popped. Remember that red wine stains.'

59

Main railway station. Pracados Trabalhadores Square. Maputo. Mozambique. 99.

I'd arrived in KwaNdukuzabo before the sun and parked on the village square. It might have confused the Italian traveller into thinking he could walk into the nearest shop and ask for an espresso. In fact, the mere thought of an espresso made me quiver with pleasure. I glanced round. I noticed that my right forearm was much browner than the other one. This was from driving with it hanging out of the window. I showed my imaginary Italian friend my dashboard, which was now a reddy-brown instead of black. I wiped across it where a large piece of masking tape had been stuck some two months ago – it still read 'One good shot a day'. Outside, the sun was rising and bleaching away at trees and poles. I turned to Makebelieve Mario and said, 'Hey, Mario, you look at real African village. You-a see many taxis coming and going. Look, people on the corner just hanging around and talking. You look and see plastic packets against fence? This is the village rose garden.' I photographed a young couple, who stood quietly, intimidated by the equipment and the powerful flash. Mario gave them each a box of Italian pasta and a bread. I leant back and found a tin of black spray paint behind my seat. 'Mario,' I said, pointing at the large billboard, 'you go and spray in big writing: "Why is the world so beautiful?"'

Don't you also want to dream of Africa, like Karen Blixen did? Or perhaps stroll onto your veranda in the early morning with a cup of tea in your hand and gaze onto endless savannah? I tried that once on a farm south of Hectorspruit. The house was situated near the summit of a hill called Vlakbultkop. I couldn't really re-enact the previous scene because I hated tea and didn't have a white colonial dressing-gown. Besides, I couldn't stroll on the veranda because I slept there. I tried the bit where the big game hunter puts his arm around the English girl's shoulder, peers into the African panorama and says, 'Isn't it beautiful, darling?' The only darling that I had had the previous night was a big Boerbul dog with a large squashed-up black face full of wrinkles. After I had managed to find my sunglasses between the many crevices of the large veranda couch, I could peer with more confidence. Man had turned the endless plains into fields of sugarcane and right through the centre of the vista ran a line of shining pylons. I gave a low visual curse, which only photographers would understand. The early morning haze was already creeping over the land. Then, in the far distance I spotted something that shocked my eyes. I steadied myself against a pillar and looked again. Was this some illusion, some mirage? A group of people, perhaps sugarcane workers, were waiting their turn to pedal on an exercise bicycle. Were the farmers getting their labourers to exercise before work? Later, when I had driven closer, I smiled – AWA, 'Africa wins again'.

Sugarcane workers sharpening Pangas. Hectorspruit area. Mpumalanga. South Africa. '99.

Retired railway worker Andries Oelofse and grandchildren Christjan and Christoffel. Watervalboven. Mpumalanga. SA.'99.

My old Elvis tape was so scratched and stretched that it sounded like he was singing all the way from heaven. There was a continuous drone on the tape, which no doubt was the humming of angels. On one cut, his voice was so distorted that he sounded like Cliff Richard. I always had to skip that section. When I stopped next to this small boy and his big rhino, Elvis and the angels were at the part where they sang, 'You've got to follow that dream wherever that dream may lead you – it's a wonderful life'. Zakele came and leant on my window, tapping his fingers to the beat. 'Please give me music', he asked with a smile that could turn white to black. On the road his older brother was waving down cars to stop at their family curio stall. There wasn't anything white that I wanted black, so I smiled back and said, 'Give me black rhino'. Zakele just laughed in disbelief. As there were no black or white rhinos in Swaziland, this was definitely the biggest dead one around. The boys' father had made it, and it stood well over a metre tall and two metres long. The tape came to the part where Elvis started to sound like Cliff Richard, so I skipped it. Zakele said, 'Give me music and car for big rhino'. Later, it was settled; Zakele got my precious Elvis tape and I got a pathetic little white rhino. So if you ever see somebody waving down the cars, and a little boy sitting next to a big black rhino, stop and listen: you'll hear Elvis singing with the angels.

Zakele with black Rhino. Near Piggs Peak. Swaziland. '99.

There's a tourist curio market on the corner of Julius Nyerere and Eduardo Mondlane avenues. We all know who Julius Nyerere was: a political visionary and spokesman for African liberation from the sixties. Bless his soul. Perhaps Eduardo was another hero of the revolution? To avoid complete harassment as a photographer, and before pointing anything anywhere, get yourself a guide from the Department of Information. If you want to photograph a scene with people in it, negotiate solely through your guide. Move slowly, downplay the situation and look completely uninterested. The streets of Maputo are the wrong place to act the flamboyant arty-farty photographer. Try to project an expression of mean friendliness. Always eat a double portion of king prawns from the Costa del Sol Hotel the previous evening. Fart at regular intervals, to keep the warriors at bay and complement the diesel fumes. Visualise your picture without looking too hard. Ask a stupid question. Point left and then move right. Not much building has taken place here since independence in 1975. If you know why, then ask why anyway. I loved the way the giant fig tree was devouring the wall. Act casual, kick a can and buy a Coke. A curio warrior comes waltzing into your frame. Through your guide, ask the dancing mask who the heck Eduardo Mondlane is. This momentarily stuns the mask into position. Take one shot and leave, in a peaceful, aggressive way.

Man in front of wild Fig tree. Julius Nyerere Avenue. Maputo. Mozambique. '99.

From the town of Barberton, road R36 curls down north-east along the Krokodilpoortberge to Kaapmuiden. The railway follows the same line as the road. This is still the same track that was laid down when the gold rush erupted in the Barberton area in 1884 and small sidings still bear the names of those wild days: 'Joe's Luck', 'Eureka' and 'Revolver Creek'. Beyond this, the mountains open out somewhat, exposing a view of the Crocodile River valley and the more distant Lowveld of the Kruger National Park. Physically, I felt good and my legs were ready to jump on anything that moved. I was visually erect, so to speak. Sadly, landscape photography was virtually impossible in the winter months. It seemed that all the farmers down the eastern side of Africa were burning their fields. Along the rivers, there were pockets of green, but most of the land was bleached and brown. I drove down the slope and crossed the bridge over Revolver Creek. There stood a group of kids with leaves tied round their ankles, dancing for the passing motorists. I decided to help them earn a better living. Firstly, we moved just beyond the bridge, to an open area in front of a dilapidated hut. This move was based on the 'Ag shame' factor. ('Ag shame, look at those poor kids trying to sing for their supper.') This factor pockets a lot more money. They practised how to look more hungry and neglected. The final move would really bring the tourists to a halt. With more leaves around their bodies now, they would crouch together to form an authentic-looking bush. As the vehicle approached, they would jump up and dance, astounding everyone in sight. That's the story of how I left behind the booming 'Revolver Creek Singing and Dancing Bush Company'.

Dancing children. Near Kaapmuiden. Mpumalanga. South Africa. '99.

I looked at the painting. It was of a chair on a stage, a little white house with smoke under a moon in the Klein Karoo. Both Wendy and her paintings evoked a kind of dream reality within me. The quality of light in her work seemed so intimate, touching and caressing all objects with love. I lifted my hands, closed my eyes and became a singer of vigorous song. Behind me the mountains replied and echoed the cheers of a tumultuous crowd. Looking through my viewfinder somehow always brings the curtain down. She was still on her back, not stroking loving light, but changing a column of smoke from left to right. I told her of all my creative thought about her dreamlike work. She clutched her chair and said, 'At least you're always doing what you do best.' I leant forward on my camera, and smiled. 'Hell, thanks, like photographing, heh?' 'Oh no,' she said, 'talking shit.' Through my viewfinder, Humphrey Bogart shrugged, from Calitzdorp, not Casablanca.

Quinine tree or Mingerhout, growing along stream near Barberton. Mpumalanga. South Africa. '99.

What a lovely experience to be able to photograph a plan that's come together. It reminded me of a friend of mine who started off selling tomatoes and ended up with – you name it. You can judge a man's success by the way he sits. Abilio reclined with a smile of achievement. I adjusted the camera height so that his arms spread along the horizon, revealing the broadness of his happiness and prosperity. (I apologise to all visual fundis that the horizon is sloping down to the left.) The warm friendly light dappled his empire, and created within me a happy glow. Little Fernando, holding the soccer ball, caused a bit of a pictorial problem. He kept on glancing at me instead of out to the distant horizon where his success might be lurking. Abilio was a shrewd businessman. He reminded me of my friend with the tomatoes. He realised that after they had all rotted, it was much easier dealing with people who wanted to buy or sell something to somebody. Abilio insisted that I would pay him for every 'clack' of the camera. (Smaller-format cameras go 'click'.) Each 'clack' would be the cost of a packet of local brand cigarettes. With more than three 'clacks', each 'clack' would then be the price of an imported packet. 'Tell me', I asked, 'how did you ever manage to start all of this?' Abilio answered with a grin, 'With one cigarette'. Somewhere there was a lesson here, along the road to Costa del Sol.

Abilio the cigarette seller. Beach near Costo del Sol Hotel. Maputo. Mozambique. '99.

In **1977**, long before Steven Spielberg had us clutching our chairs and each other in Jurassic Park, a mere mortal called Jan van Zyl made a dinosaur park outside the Sudwala Caves. These caves are situated on the side of a mountain which the locals call 'Mankelekele' (probably Shangaan, meaning 'Crag on Crag'). After six in the evening, I watched the last of the visitors leave. It was one of those wonderful Afrikaans families that Spielberg could use as extras in a future movie called *Gondwanaland's God*. (It would be an epic in which Nelson Mandela returns from heaven as a saint to sort out all the wars, corruption, crime and other bullshit in southern Africa.) The mother was big, walked with a positive step, and swung her bottom just enough for no one to get any pleasurable thoughts. Three little boys, all with cupped ears, freckles and crewcuts, ran around the prehistoric beasts shouting 'Kyk-hier-kyk-hier-kyk-hier'. The father, with a slight stoop, followed her obediently, three metres behind. The last of the sun stroked the hills, crevices deepened in blue, and quiet came to Mankelekeleland. I sat down on poor Brontosaurus, still shivering out the last spasms of life, after being viciously attacked by Tyrannosaurus. One of the boys with the cupped ears and freckles came running past, crying for his mother. I looked at Tyrannosaurus and smiled. Then, silence again in Gondwanaland, with just faint sounds of Diplodocus chewing leaves from a nearby pond.

Tyrannosaurus killing Brontosaurus. Dinosaur Park. Sudwala Caves. Mpumalanga. South Africa. '99.

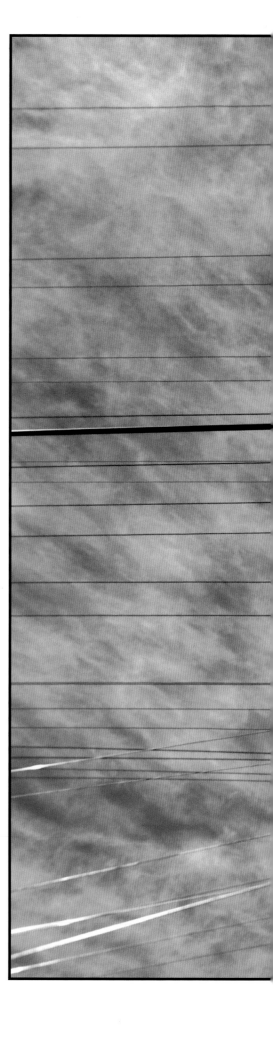

Telkom worker walking in the sky between Barberton and Kaapmuiden. Mpumalanga. South Africa. '99.

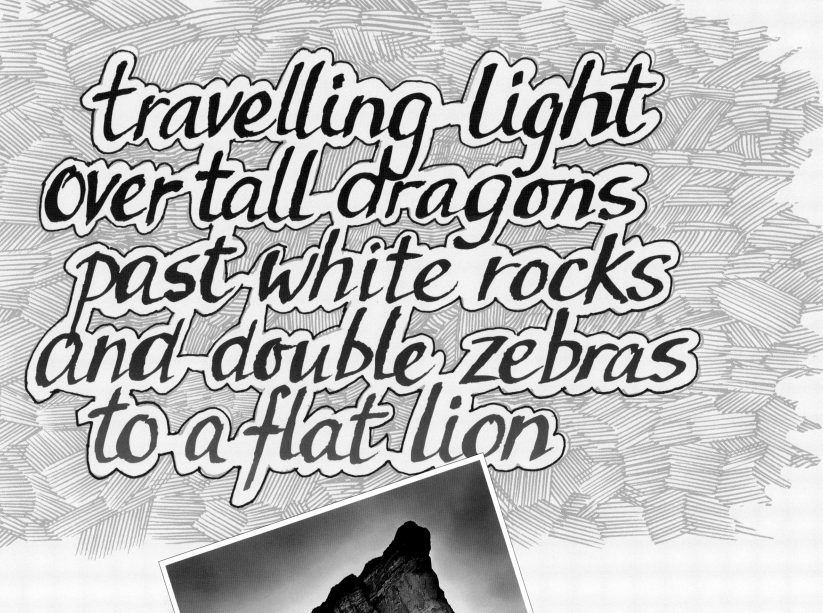

travelling light
over tall dragons
past white rocks
and double zebras
to a flat lion

Three months after I had photographed the tree, I managed to trace an article that appeared in a Natal newspaper on 17 March 1947: 'It was again overcast and inclined to drizzle but there was still an air of excitement amongst everyone as the highlight of the day was to be the tree planting ceremony near the swimming pool to commemorate the Royal Family's visit. The king sent a message that as they had appreciated no photographers, they would allow photographs of the tree planting for the hotel's personal records. At 12.30 p.m. their Majesties arrived and the ceremony began. The King, Queen and both Princesses each planted a Natal Yellowwood tree (*Podocarpus henkelii*). The trees were planted in turn, with each shovelling two or three spades of earth around the tree whilst posing for the amateur photographers. During the afternoon there was a men's doubles tennis set in which the King participated. It was a very homely scene as Princess Margaret took a cine of them playing and Princess Elizabeth fagged balls.'

Yellowwood tree planted by Queen Elizabeth. Royal Natal National Park. KwaZulu-Natal. South Africa. '99.

Early morning. Golden Gate National Park. Eastern Free State. South Africa.

When it comes to computers, I am a complete *poephol* [arsehole]. This is because I hate the thought of sitting in a room peering at a screen. My computer is in my head, and it is programmed to record small situations in a broad African way. I am, so to speak, computer literate in a weird and travelling kind of way. My mouse is my hands on the steering wheel and I can click on anywhere from Babanango to Swartwitspensbokfonteinberg. Getting to some places is often a Hard Drive. So driving around with this thing in my head is wonderful, as I can not only view it, but sense it, touch it, hear it and smell it. Imagine my excitement as I drove around a corner in the hills of Maganganguzi and saw people covered in white cloths sitting near white rocks. Automatically the computer showed 'Calm down, over-excited photographers bungle matters'. I saw a chap waving his hands and holding a book in his hand. He was dressed in traditional Zulu garments. I clicked my mouse on him. 'Sipho Mangele, head priest of the Nazareth Baptist Church, PO Box 193, Loskop 3330'. The computer added, 'Exclude him, photograph the white rocks and figures'. I moved my mouse over and clicked on the figures. Out came 'AmaXhosa Zana, unmarried holy children'. I clicked on the little girl without a cloth. Computer screen: 'Stupid question, arsehole, she forgot hers at home'. I clicked on the white stones. Computer: 'Mnyangweni, holy stones. Stop asking so much and get on with the bloody job'. So I got out the car, took off my shoes, entered the holy circle, and photographed the holy rocks with the holy children on the holy ground near Maganganguzi.

AmaXhosa Zana – unmarried holy children. Nazareth Baptist Church. Near Maganganguzi. South Africa. '99.

Young Witchdokter woman. Near Mpompolwane. KwaZulu-Natal. South Africa. '99.

Ardmore Guest Farm lies in the Champagne Valley beneath some of the highest peaks in southern Africa. It is a rustic place with thatched rondavels and a well-known ceramic studio set amongst trees in a large garden. My vista was wide, high and broad. In the left foreground, the massive trunk of an old bluegum tree lay where it had fallen twenty years ago. As the haze controlled the distant, I had to busy myself with the near. I called the four housekeeping ladies, and posed Thandi at the back and mother Lefina Shabalala holding her daughter in the front. In the centre stood 20-year-old Tholokele Mazibuko. She had just had her first baby; her first name 'Tholokele' means, in Zulu, 'We'll get another one'.

Housekeeping ladies. Ardmore Guest Farm. Champagne Valley. KwaZulu-Natal. South Africa. '99.

I **grew up on a small farm** outside Pretoria. One day, my father sat me down across from him at the dining-room table. He looked at me in his soft, gentle way and said, 'So this is what you want, son, to leave the NG Kerk? Because you took your little black friend to church and the Dominee told him to wait outside?' So it came about that a young boy did what he had to do, all those 40 years ago. I stopped playing 'Kaffir en Polisie' and could shake a black man's hand without feeling awkward. Sadly, though, the political tides of those years littered most of us so-called Europeans with the flotsam of racial prejudice and superior philosophies. The great tide of racial domination came and swept our little naïve bits of wood away and made us float unconcerned, blind, privileged, over this sad land. The good God-fearing Afrikaners and the friendly fair English went to church to love their neighbours like themselves. Then we all went home to have drinks, braai chops on the fire and discuss the *swart gevaar*, the communist onslaught, world isolation and how the cricketer Basil D'Oliveira was used as a political pawn. Some of us thought about our bits of wood, still floating somewhere in the Ocean of Wrong. Then we went to university to have a great time, wear Che Guevara berets, hum Beatles songs and, when we had had too many drinks, agree that everything the government did was shit. Then, many years later, the tide brought Nelson Mandela from prison and the colour of the ocean changed somewhat. Our little bits of flotsam became bigger, better, and we told people, whilst grilling our chops, how we used to swim against the racial current, political wrongs and evil security police, and that Basil D'Oliveira was a great batsman. When we had had one too many chops, we felt for the underprivileged, put on the old beret and promised to vote ANC the next time round.

Herbalist shop. Bergville. KwaZulu-Natal province. South Africa. '99.

Temporary dining room tent. Franschhoek Mt. Lodge. Witteberge. Eastern Free State. South Africa. '99.

There is a belief amongst some art philosophers that photography should document, as faithfully as possible, the world around us. Others, on the contrary, say that if this is done, images will become over-complicated, cluttered and, in many instances, boring. They feel one should bring some structure and order to a chaotic and complex visual world; in other words, isolate and detach with smaller pictorial elements to amplify the larger issues. This again, in turn, would not be truthful, and might deceive the viewer into misconceptions. In this photograph the fact is that the Franschhoek Mountain Lodge burnt down, and to accommodate the guests they put up a tent. Once inside the tent, there was visual warfare – because opposite colours fight. The turquoise was having it out with the orange. The poor old lion that had been walked on since the 1920s was now elevated from under the table to the top of the table in the '90s. I then asked Mapoledisa and Blandina to join him. They felt awkward as the table was for guests, not for them and a lion. If a photographer wants to be cool and collected he must practise shooting lions with awkward people. Japie and Vincent joined us. A wide-angle lens close to the lion's head enlarged its size, and reduced Japie to the size of a glass. He liked that and asked if there was something nice inside the glass. Photographers which do not want to record the world faithfully, but rather make the obvious absurd, should practise with fighting colours, awkward lions and something nice in a glass.

Dragon Peaks Holiday Resort. Drakensberg mountains. KwaZulu-Natal. South Africa '99.

Golden Gate National Park. Eastern Free State. South Africa. '99.

Local women chopping up cattle heads. Near KwaMiya. KwaZulu-Natal Drakensberg. South Africa. '99.

The road from KwaMiya makes a steep curve and turns into the main road from Zwelitsha on a sharp bend. From there it does one more kink, then levels out and becomes a straight road. A straight road with a kink after a steep curve on a sharp bend would summarise nicely what travel is like in the hinterland – a criss-cross pattern of unpredictability. To this roadish broth, you now add the fermented mix of race, colour, culture, creed and eleven official languages. When it rains, it usually pours along with hail, haze, mud, blood and scorching drought, which affects everyone including some corrupt officials, good crooks and some rotten cops. The one moment we're all Hunkies and Dories, screaming together for Bafana Bafana to at least equalise, before our dream rainbow disappears. On the other hand, we couldn't give a shit about Hunky and Dory, and laugh our heads off at some corrupt officials, good crooks, rotten cops and the mampara of the week. So, with padded absurdity and a little rainbow flag, I travel over the potholes in road's kinks, missing a cow, ox, horse, mule, sheep, goat and 87 taxis. I am not at all surprised when there's a thunder flash from a dark cloud and I swerve for a dog and a cat. So there's nothing strange and squeamish when you look from the steep curve on the sharp bend and see twelve ladies hacking away at twelve cattle heads in the middle of nowhere between KwaMiya and Zwelitsha.

It's a good couple of years ago that the QwaQwa people were also given their little patch of the quilt to live on. Their little homeland straddles the Maluti Mountains, where they meet the Natal Drakensberg. Later, when parts of the national quilt were starting to burn, QwaQwa's capital, Witsieshoek, changed quietly one evening to Phuthaditjhaba. It was from here that I drove into the mountains with the day farewelling the west and evening advancing from the east. I drove into the mountains with both windows open, sharing the spirits of both. When day became half-night, I photographed myself, travelling light, where the cliffs hang over a kink in the road.

Road to Witsieshoek Mountain Inn. Maluti Mountains. Free State. South Africa. '99.

Brandtwag Buttress. Golden Gate Highlands National Park. Free State. South Africa. '99.

Sibusiso can fly. Sibusiso's heart is high in the sky and it flies around the mountain tops alone, where the eagles are. His arms are the wings that soar on the currents of air that start around the hills of his village, and breathe upwards, pushing columns of cloud around the peaks. At first he did not realise that he could fly; only the swallows that streaked across the sky chasing flying ants after the rain, flew; or the cranes that landed so slowly, like the old aeroplanes he had in his book, to feed in the field below his father's hut. Then, one day, he heard the sound of the big bird that clever people had made, far across the mountains. The aeroplane emerged from behind the blue mountain and roared over his village with wings of steel. It was from that day, after the chickens had flapped across the yard and the cattle had stampeded over the fields, that Sibusiso's heart became the wings of a plane. Now he was already 29 years old, and the years had flown in many ways over his village against the hills. Some were dry years, others happy and glad years, when he could dip his wings and look down on the green mealie fields. Each day he works on building his planes, and every evening he pulls up the stairs to his house in a plane. I look up from my table at home, and from the ceiling hang two of Sibusiso's planes: the one is red and the other blue; and when the wind from the window makes them move, I can once again imagine him flying.

Sibusiso Mbhele – plane maker. Near Zwelitsha village. KwaZulu-Natal. South Africa. '99.

Near Witsieshoek Mountain Inn. Drakensberg. KwaZulu-Natal. South Africa. '99.

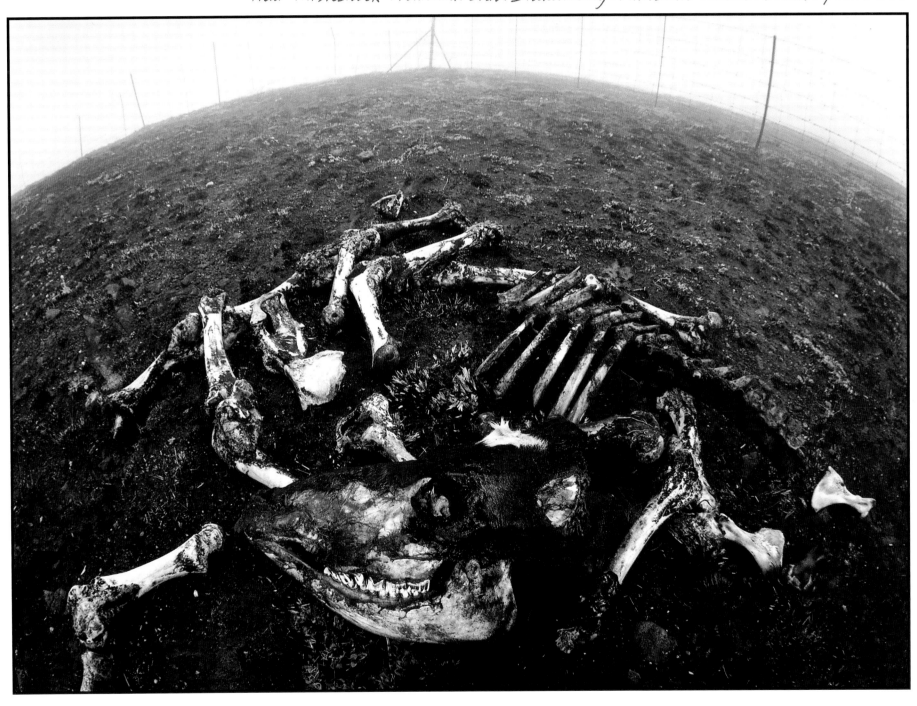

from a moffie dog
monty the python
a few good students
in a city of saints
and some sinners

Evening exposure. The Owl House. Nieu Bethesda. Eastern Cape. South Africa. '99.

View from Rhodes University clock tower down High Street. Grahamstown. Eastern Cape. South Africa. '99.

95

Looking towards the Cathedral. Bathurst Street. Grahamstown. Eastern Cape. South Africa. 2000.

Photography section. Rhodes University. Grahamstown. Eastern Cape. South Africa. '99.

Margaret. Rhodes University service staff. Grahamstown. Eastern Cape. South Africa. 2000

Scene from play – "iMumbo Jumbo." Grahamstown. Eastern Cape. South Africa. 97.

I lie behind the curtains on the stage of the NG church hall, exercising, and listen to my wife Lynn drone out her instructions to her callanetics class. I force myself to attend her classes because through various physical and mental excesses my body and mind are in rather bad shape. Her body and mind are in such good shape that it makes me have lengthy conversations with the big man that hovers above me at the back of the stage. He's given me such wonderful advice that I would like to express my deepest thanks to him and Lynn by including them in this book.

The church hall ghost watching Lynn's callanetics class relaxing.

Witches in a scene from "Ipi Zombi". Outside Grahamstown. Eastern Cape. South Africa. 2000.

Flock of geese walking past old trucks. Market Street. Grahamstown. Eastern Cape. South Africa. 2000

Basil Mills lives in his own empire with his family at Donkerbosch Outspan outside Grahamstown. The road that snakes down to his house, past old wagons, a horse carriage and a couple of old cannons, is adventurous and, of course, fairly shit. I wave to his wife, busy saddling up her white horse. On her hip she is wearing a leather holster with bullets and a Colt revolver. I am so thrilled to be back in the mid-1800s that I almost collide with Basil's pet ox. As I dismount from my old car, I spot a blue blur chasing a red blur: Basil's two sons. The one is wearing war-paint and the other a raccoon cape – probably Hiawatha and Davy Crockett. Knowing Basil is a passionate romantic, a lover of legends of old, an adventurer with a pioneering spirit, you realise that the two boys, who are now peacefully sitting in a tree, are old Eastern Cape enemies, taking a break. Inside the house I busy myself clearing a visual passage for a portrait through all the paraphernalia of bygone days. Basil is playing with his tarantula. I know that he is a founder member of SABRE – the South African Battle Re-enactment Society – and takes children out on adventure education camps, linking South African literature and nature, with themes varying from pirates and shipwreck trails, to 1820 settler wagon camps. He can frequently be found taking interested parties to Olive Schreiner's mountain tomb overlooking the plains of the Karoo in-between tracking down Tom the rhino at his hideout in the Thomas Baines nature reserve. I decide to photograph him with one of his pets – the warthog, the owl, the boa constrictor. How about him sitting on his ox surrounded by all his stuff? 'No', Basil replies, 'this isn't a china shop and the ox would be upset because he's no longer a bull!' I settle for Basil and Monty the python.

Rasta Oberholzer, the Weimaraner dog. Donkin Street. Grahamstown. Eastern Cape. South Africa. 2000.

Colonel Konrad Most was one of the world's most famous and distinguished authorities on all types of dog-training and a pioneer in the study of dog psychology. He was the head of the Canine Service of the German Army High Command in the two great wars. In 1931 he founded the German Society for Animal Psychology. In his many books, he based his training on the principle that treated the dog, not as an intelligent human pupil imbued with a sense of duty, but as an animal, beyond good or evil, living in a world without moral values and learning not by logical thinking but solely through the faculty of memory. This system avoids the mistake of endowing dogs with human understanding and morals – a mistake which renders any real partnership between man and dog so difficult. To Colonel Most, who died in 1954, I'd like to send a posthumous apology: 'Dear Colonel, the greatest of my failures has been that towards my beloved Weimaraner dogs. They think they are humans, kiss me, eat from my plate, growl at bad art, talk to the full moon and sleep in my bed. So, dear Colonel, I hope that you don't turn in your grave too often and please accept my sincerest apologies from me down in this dog world. It's too late for change now. Yours truly ... Obie Oberholzer.'

Car guard waiting. High Street Square. Grahamstown. Eastern Cape. South Africa. 2000.

In my opinion Professor Andrew Buckland is the best-known personality residing in the City of Saints at present. I am convinced that he's also sinned. I asked him to write his own caption. 'Andrew Buckland, pictured here in the infamous water suit from his play *The Water Juggler*, is an actor, teacher and general all-round *doos* who wishes he was a musician or a famous photographer so that he could travel around Africa in a fancy car like Obie. The water juggler is a play about a man, Jerry Can Do, and his journey through a landscape of drought, desert, blood-sucking wattles, magical water creatures and witches who live at the bottom of wells. The suit is sold to him as "an intercontinental ballistic drain gun with diverter gaskets which gives it thermal relief-combat capabilities. It has partition-mounted dip tubes, an active infrared hose adaptor and pressure-regulated reverse osmosis in the aerator. You see some extension tank rolling towards you? You just flip up the slip-jointed rings on the flush-valve interceptor over to anti-syphon and you are sitting in a high-speed, anti-insulation, pump-action tactical bowl guard that is virtually indestructible." Born and schooled in Zimbabwe, Andrew studied at Rhodes in the seventies and worked as a freelance performer in Johannesburg for eleven or twelve years before returning to Rhodes in 1992. He is best known for some humiliating television commercials and for his particular brand of physical, comic and satirical style of animation theatre which uses mime techniques to overcome the fact that, despite living in South Africa for twenty-three years, he is still unilingual. He is married to Janet, who is the proud owner of the grandson of one of Obie's Weimaraners.'

Basil's tame ox watching Sylvia carrying her load. Stoneshill. Eastern Cape. South Africa. '99.

An advertising agency from Cape Town asked me if I would photograph a scene for a well-known international removals company. Part of the ad's text would read: 'This may look odd. But it's full of practicality and efficiency. The old African tradition of carrying heavy loads on the head puts less strain on the body and allows people to move things further.' I am normally slightly apprehensive of flashy young art directors – an advanced species of creative human beings that have elevated visual, humoristic and verbal capabilities. The young man who flew in from Cape Town was, however, enthusiastic, helpful and understanding. First we designed our African load from objects around my house. With this load and camera equipment, we proceeded in the Kombi to collect my camera assistant and my Xhosa translator. Then on to Joza township where we picked up Sylvia, who had been pre-selected for her Xhosa elegance and load-carrying capabilities. On the first day we photographed around the hills of Grahamstown and the rural communities beyond the Fish River. The following day, Basil Mills's help was called in. 'Great,' shouted the art director, 'a tame African ox in the picture ... wow!' So with Basil's ox on his bakkie we rumbled our way up to his *lapa*, which overlooked the coastal landscape. Matthew, my translator, had nothing to translate, so he was happy sitting under a tree. However, although usually quite plentiful, we couldn't find a Xhosa baby on the mountain, so the art director made one out of two pillows. The clouds rolled in, Matthew sat, Brent flashed, the art director smiled, I shot, and that's how it came about that Basil's tame ox watched Sylvia carrying her load.

Excerpts from an interview published in *Artreach* a while ago, with play director Brett Bailey of The Third World Bunfight HQ, who says: 'When one or more performers are doing their thing with their entire being, with skill and talent, a whole room of people may be transported beyond themselves ... As mouthpieces of a newly united collective trying to find its feet, we need to challenge the inherited conventions which have bound us and our ways of thinking and expressing. We have to take risks to push the boundaries outwards. As a white man I have aroused some black anger by writing and directing plays with Xhosa themes and their collision with the West. *Mumbo Jumbo* told the story of Chief Gcaleka's trip to Britain to retrieve the skull of King Hintsa. *Ipi Zombi?* recounts the saga of witch-hunting and hysteria which turned Kokstad's Bhongweni township on its head after twelve schoolboys died in a Kombi crash in 1995. But I have also had a lot of positive feedback ... One of my aims is to make drama that touches people right across the social spectrum. Why should journalists who have the sketchiest background knowledge about events be able to sensationalise stories while artists, who throw themselves into deep research, are condemned for trespassing in another culture? Such criticisms do not even interest me. Theatre should take risks, tell the stories, and reflect the moods of the land ... The Eastern Cape has such historical cultural wealth: powerful and moving songs and dances, rich and unusual folkstories and histories, ancient customs and beliefs, which tell of a society much healthier than the one South Africans now share.'

Scene from Brett Bailey's play – 'Ipi Zombi'. Grahamstown Festival. Eastern Cape. South Africa. ±'97.

just one more in the bar
next to the church
to welcome and welcome
baardskeerdersbos horses
moonrise over graves

Shot and skinned domestic hunting dogs. Near Swellendam. Western Cape. South Africa. '99.

The mist hovered over the road, which came from Bredasdorp and stretched out till it crossed the road coming from Protem and going to Renosterfontein. The sign had fallen down and the old bullet holes through it had made long streaks of brown rust. It looked like it was crying. I thought that I would cheer it up and give the old holes some new friends. This could easily be done by shooting some new ones next to the old. The shots scared the ostrich (which had been standing next to the yield sign watching me). Not much later, the sun and Gert Jacobs appeared almost simultaneously. I wondered which was stranger, Gert and the sun, the ostrich at a yield sign, or a weeping Renosterfontein sign. Gert Jacobs asked me if I had a job for him. That depended, I said, on whether he could tell me when last he had seen a group of rhinoceros standing round a spring. No, he definitely hadn't seen anything as funny as that. Only, an ostrich, running his gat af [arse off], back and forth across a field.

113

Farm labourer houses. Riviersonderend Mountains. Overberg district. Western Cape. South Africa. '99.

Theewaterskloof dam with Franschhoek Mts. Near Villiersdorp. Overberg district. Western Cape. South Africa. '99.

It was going to be one of those days that already start to bubble long before breakfast. The wind was light, exactly east, and pulling clouds from the sunshine over the fynbos mountains near Napier. I could smell the light around me. A dog charged, barking, then stopped and stared. The men had already left, to work in the flower fields on Tolbos farm. You know, sometimes you get lucky, if you go with the sun and the wind. Tina had on jeans and wore the pants in the house. She helped me organise the shot. Sam and James goofed around in the front. Marie looked good against the green, Maria put her arm around Wessels, and young Priscilla pushed in little Leta's cheeks to make her smile. For a short little while, the sad were happy in Happysadland.

Williams and Standaard families. Tolbos flower farm. Near Napier. Overberg. Western Cape. South Africa. '99.

Snoekies Groenewald. Horse trainer and farmer. Baardskeerdersbos. Western Cape. South Africa. '99.

I felt that a few eyes were trailing me, as if stroking the back of my head, as I walked through the village. Shapes moved behind curtained windows, some dirty, others covered with old lace. Baardskeerdersbos was small, and I soon found Snoekies Groenewald in the stables outside his small house. 'No, Mister', he said, 'we don't trust you journalist types. You come in here with your open smiling faces. Then, later, you go away and write a lot of *kak* things about us people here. Why don't you just go away ...' He turned round and looked towards his beloved horses and the fields that ran down to the Boesmans River. A little later, after we had spoken about horses, I could feel him soften and become like the good earth around him. He was born in 1939, in the Caledon area. During the '50s and early '60s he roamed the Strandveld as a shepherd, earning 14 shillings a month. He said, in a proud voice, 'My great love is training horses. In my time, I have trained 3050 horses.' So, as promised, no *kak* about Baardskeerdersbos.

White horse looking east away from sunset. Bredasdorp. Overberg. Western Cape. South Africa. '99.

Position the camera as close to the horse as possible. By virtue of simple perspective and viewpoint, the horse is now as big as the grain silos that stand across the railway lines in Bredasdorp. In actual fact, the capacity of a single silo is 1600 tons of grain, and that of a horse half a bale of hay. The art philosopher will add that the gentle curve of the horse's back amplifies the rigidity of the silos, while the warm foreground light contrasts with the whimsical blue hues of the sky. At the same time the compositional pushing of the horse to the right of the frame emphasises the difference between the monumental man-made structures and the quiet flow of the natural world. What really happened was that in positioning the camera and tripod, I stepped on a big heap of horseshit. The thick green stuff oozed into my sandals and between my toes. This made me scream such obscene and disgusting swearwords that the horse looked away to the east whilst the sun quietly sank down in the west.

Farmlands along the Langeberge near Swellendam. Overberg. Western Cape. South Africa. '99.

Paardekloof farm along the Witsand—Heidelberg road. Overberg district. Western Cape. South Africa. '99.

Leon Binneman shaking hands with Andries Auret. Napier. Overberg. Western Cape. South Africa. '99.

There is a saying in Afrikaans that goes, 'Die kerk en die bar is langs mekaar [The church and the bar are next to each other]'. This means, in a maner of speaking, that drinking is bad and praying is good. Take this interpretation even further and you could come up with God and the Devil, salvation and damnation. These advanced philosophies came to me after my third double brandy and Coke, in the bar across from the church. The barmaid said that in Napier the Devil drove a red Volkswagen Beetle. A while later, when a warm light had descended on the town, I managed to get Leon Binneman to shake hands with Andreis Auret, the hotel owner and the Dominee. Oom Kotie came rumbling down the main road in his 1975 Ford truck. When he saw all this handshaking he stopped and asked, 'Ek sê, why the hell is the Dominee shaking hands with the bottlestore owner?' 'Because', Leon answered, 'die kerk en die bar is mos langs mekaar'.

Main street through Elim village. Overberg district. Western Cape. South Africa '99

Moonrise over graves of 6 children who drowned at Witsand (15.12.96). Bredasdorp. Western Cape. South Africa. '99.

Anneline Thomas

Lilian Strydom

Mien Tiennie

Caroline Jacobs

Van der Berg

Henry Strydom

Indian Ocean before dawn. Rocks at Arniston. Overberg district. Western Cape. South Africa. '99.

Sunrise over Atlantic near Arniston. Overberg. Western Cape. South Africa. '99.

It was really still quite dark. At this time, human eyes have an inexplicable frailty. Or that's how it seemed as the light moved across the waves. The camera's time exposure can make the dimness brighter. In the vastness, opposites were struggling with each other: red sky and blue sea; wet, dry; cold, warm. The waves came in and out, and in again. 'Whoosh, whoosh,' said the round rocks. I bent down and touched a rock. It sent a ripple up my spine, through my mind, into my eye.

Isak Karelse, Hermanus Dreyers, Samuel Martinus. Retired fishermen. Arniston. Western Cape. South Africa. '99.

The girls stood in the door and the kids played on the wall. Samuel chuckled, then put his hands on his old friend's shoulders. 'Ja, Hermanus, where have all those strong muscles gone?' 'God will know that', answered Izak Karelse, 'and knows that the muscles have gone away, like most of the fish. God knows, how long did we fish that great ocean? You, Samuel ... 50 years. And me, what was it? 25 years. You, Hermanus, 55 years, the longest of us all. God will know that.'

Cape Agulhas lighthouse. Overberg. Western Cape. South Africa. '99.

'Dammit,' I said, stopping the car by the water, the mist. It was early morning. The road to Witsand is broken by the river and the pont at Malgas. The pontoniers, following tradition, work between sunrise and sunset. This alone was a problem. Where was the sun? Was it up? Another problem was that the pont wasn't even visible – on the other side of the river, not this side. What's more, the pont at Malgas doesn't just come when you call it. From previous crossings I knew, or at least hoped, that Welcome Ngardo and Welcome Bota still operated the pont. If they couldn't see the sun, they might still be asleep under the tree. I cupped my hands round my mouth and shouted, 'Welcome!' A flock of ducks took off from the reeds. 'Welcome … come!' A voice without a body shouted back through the mist, 'Welcome. Welcome coming.'

'Welcome' Ngardo and 'Welcome' Bota. Malgas pontoon workers. Overberg. Western Cape. South Africa. '99.

Pierre van Zyl. Cape Agulhas lighthouse keeper with Robert Arendse. Overberg district. Western Cape. South Africa. '99.

Pierre van Zyl, the lighthouse-keeper, looked down. The setting sun made him glow warm orange. The sky behind was so blue that it actually hurt. His assistant, Robert Arendse, leant on the glass, near the lighthouse lens. The camera was pointing due south. We were very near to the most southern point in Africa. It was 5 June 1999, the time on his watch read 17.35 hours and 35 seconds. On his forearm, he had what looked like a tattoo of a mermaid. I exposed for one-fifteenth of a second at an aperture of f22. 'Thanks a lot', I said, '... and where else have you been lighthousing?' The sun was setting fast. Pierre looked at it, screwing up his eyes. 'All of them', he answered, 'all, except one, to hell 'n' gone north of St Lucia ... there near Cape Vidal. It gets too lonely out there ...' The sun set: it was 17.55 and 6 seconds.

Road to Infanta along the Brede River near Malgas. Overberg district. Western Cape. South Africa. '99.

This is a two-hour exposure begun at what one could describe as twilight time. Over a period of time, modern emulsions have developed the ability to record detail even in the darkest of scenes. When the light starts to fade, not many cars drive to Cape Infanta, around the corner, where the Breede River makes a turn. Four times I drove, back and forth, around Breede Bend, up to a hill where the road makes a swing. The river breathed coolness along the banks of the land. I drove a while with my hazard lights on, then stopped across the way from a house that looked so very much like a house – so nice, one red roof, two rooms, two windows and steps leading up to a door. Here I am, I thought, tapping a beat on the dashboard, in Haphazardland, looking right, looking left, to a house on a hill, where the road swings round the river's bend.

Moravian Church ladies in front of Royal Café. Elim village. Overberg. Western Cape. South Africa. '99.

children at moedverloor
finding harry hantam
past the mayor's balls
to a dark sky
where the gannets fly

Road Kill. Dead buck between Brandvlei and Loeriesfontein. Northern Cape. South Africa. '99.

It's a road, a gravel one, a damn long road between Brandvlei and Loeriesfontein. The *bossies* and *koppies* go by and blur with the dust behind the car. The big Karoo becomes pockets of thought, visual doodles, clouds of memories. An insect splats its grease on the windscreen, exactly where the land meets the sky. You line it up, to the road's vanishing point – and drive it over the horizon. You're so awake that you're almost asleep, and drive the car with your heart. A farmer's sign comes and goes, and you wonder whether you should shoot a couple of bullet holes through it, or drive into his farm and ask whether you could use his toilet. The only reason for this is that you want to be in a small room and not a car, spray some of the rose-petal fragrance around, and read in *You* magazine how a wife discovered the darker side of her husband. Later the sun moves slowly down to the west and all the shapes push their shadows out, away from the evening light. It occurred to me again, as so many times before, that freedom is knowing not quite where one is going. Even if you're on the road between Brandvlei and Loeriesfontein.

Flattened Coke tin along the road to Moordenaarskloof. Near Calvinia. Northern Cape. South Africa. '99.

Looking down towards Moordenaarskloof. Hantam Karoo. Northern Province. South Africa. '99.

According to legend 'Moordenaarspoort' received its name from a sad incident that happened many years ago. Two groups of Bushmen lived on two adjoining farms, Welbedacht and Spitskop. A great passion of love developed between a married woman and a young man from the two different clans. This fuelled hostilities between the groups, ending in a fight. Almost all the men from both groups of Bushmen died, and where burned by the women from both clans buried their fallen men. The group of stones marking their graves can still be seen today.

You can enter Nieuwoudtville from Calvinia on the R27 or from the Loeriesfontein side. It doesn't really matter, as the main street is called Voortrekker Street and is absolutely straight. This gives one the fabulous opportunity to spend a great deal of time looking left and right. The church and the café, the hotel, the co-op, the garage and the cops. Absolutely fabulous! Don't you get pissed off with people who continuously say 'fabulous' and 'absolutely'? I parked the car, and just sat. Then I wondered whether I should go to the bar and get drunk. Who knows, I might meet the mayor there, or perhaps 'Miss Nieuwoudtville's' brother. Wouldn't that be absolutely fabulous? In fact it was so fabulous sitting in Voortrekker Street looking straight, and then left and then right, that I could lower my seat another notch. I must have dozed off a while, because when I looked left again a man was staring at me from behind a gate. 'Can I help you?' he shouted. 'Are you lost?' I noticed that he had a fabulous face. When he put his hands on the gate I glanced away to the right. 'No, I'm not lost', I shouted back, 'I am looking for Harry Hantam'. His happy face turned into a puzzled one. 'No, Mister, I am Jan Golly. There is no Harry Hantam here'. Then I took his photograph, wished him well, and drove out along Voortrekker Street. Golly fabulous.

Small 'Bakkies' boats in Lambertsbay harbour. Atlantic coastline. Western Cape. South Africa. '99.

Groenrivier ruins. Nieuwoudtville. Northern Cape. South Africa. '99.

When a car is a bike, and a house is a hut, when the stove needs wood, the kettle has dents and love means a lot – you're there, at Melkhoutboskraal. Winters mean frost and summers mean sweat, sheep are for shearing and seldom to eat. Love is for children, and a husband, a wife and, most of all, for God – who sometimes forgets to provide. When a bike gets you far, a hut is enough, *twak* [tobacco] is gold, and when the gold in your teeth pays for a coffin to heaven – you'll know you're there. Send my regards to them all – at Melkhoutboskraal.

Post office workers, Sarina, Sarie, Koemien and Bradley. Calvinia. Hantam Karoo. Northern Province. South Africa. '99.

When I was a young boy, I was scared of postboxes. I thought that when you put a letter through the slit, a monster would grab you and suck you inside. This was a terrifying thought, because all foreign mail first went to Pommieland [England] on the mail boat that took four weeks. Finally, after enduring all this, some large postbox would spit you out in some strange dismal country, as thin as a boy from the British concentration camps. I hated postboxes because in those years most of them looked so pompous, so British. Then, suddenly, on 14 July 1999, I forgave and forgot, and photographed the biggest postbox in the world (height: 6,17 metres; circumference: 9,43 m; and volume: 436,132 m^3). In front Sarina, with the dark hair, held Sarie, with the red hair, and on her right was Komien, with the blonde hair. They all smiled, loved their husbands and worked happily in the post office. In front of the postbox, postman Bradley posed proudly.

De Hoop Cottage. Papkuilsfontein Farm. Nieuwoudtville. Northern Province. South Africa. '99.

Freddie Koopman and friends. Wuppertal Mission village. Cederberg. Cape Province. South Africa. '99.

In Paris, during the 1920s, a new way of photographic 'seeing' began to take hold. Cameramen started to question the established norms of looking. They challenged the view of man standing on his two feet looking straight ahead. They moved things, changed viewpoints, manipulated prints, photographed down from above and up from below. They homed in on small things, extended large ones, humorised, abstracted the mundane and isolated for the sake of impact. Rocks became breasts, sand dunes sensual, roots became hungry, water reflected thoughts and, for many, the world changed and became forever different.

147

Once you're past Wuppertal, the road becomes narrow and winds along the Tratraberge. Soon I reached a point where I could stop and look down on Beukeskraal. It lies in something of a hollow along the river, and shows a couple of old white cottages along the dusty road. At the entrance there is a large kraal, which appeared to have a couple of young goats in it. A little further along the narrow main road, something strange was happening. I squinted my eyes and looked again. Small beings with big heads were jumping around in jerky stop-start movements. I counted about twenty of them; all had blue-green heads. Then I wrote in my journal: 'Day 201. 18th July 1999. Time: 16.45 hrs. Place: Earth. Position: 19°17' East 30°20' South. Situation: Grave. Alien-like beings have landed. Strange activity.' Then I drove down to the village and found the children of Beukeskraal playing hopscotch along the dusty main road.

ME (looking into the pigsty): 'Howzit, pig.'

PIG (waking up): '... Oink ...'

ME (placing camera): 'Wow, you've got big ones.'

PIG (puzzled): 'Oink?'

ME (focusing lens): 'Tits.'

PIG (angry): 'Oink! Oink!'

ME (setting aperture): 'You're a mother.'

PIG (nodding): 'O-I-I-nnn-k.'

ME (1/30th of a second at f16): 'Grubby kids, hey?'

PIG (advancing): 'Oink, oink, oink.'

ME (checking focus): 'You know what?'

PIG (staring): 'Oink?'

ME (exposing): 'Bacon for breakfast.'

PIG (upset): 'O-i-i-i-nnk.'

ME (rewinding film): 'Sorry.'

PIG (sulking): 'Oink.'

ME (leaving): 'Pig's day, Mom, and thanks.'

Pig and house at sunrise. Wuppertal Mission village. Cederberg. Western Cape. South Africa. '99.

Life can be lonely and sad. 'We pass through each other's lives and fade into the past.' Ouma Koba sat in her kitchen and held Oortjies close. How does the saying go? 'Time changes everything.' Beyond her smile was a book of memories – the laughter of children, singing, crying, the clatter of life, people talking, arriving, leaving, living. Ouma Koba stroked Oortjies. First she had given birth to Evely and Eva, then Gert, and Johanna, and Koos, and then Chrisjan, and Andries, then Katrin, and Michael, then Hennie and Koti. There were eleven of them all in all, but one day Eva died, which left her with ten. Then the rest left home, married, loved and had 26 children, who grew up, and lived and loved, and each time they brought Ouma Koba a newborn face to see. The children brought the grandchildren, and the grandchildren brought the great-grandchildren – 56 children in all. Ouma Koba hugged Oortjies and smiled.

79-year-old Ouma Koba Jantjies. Grootmoedverloor village. Northern Cape. South Africa. '99

I **counted seven of them** – hadeda birds flying home over the tortured pinnacle rocks of the eastern Cederberg range. The western sky turned cool violet, and around me the rocks seemed to groan out their collected daily warmth. The cracks and crevices spoke in whispers. Dimness was changing to darkness, hadeda cries to the squeals of flying shapes. I entered the passages of the City Hall Caves, passing into the dark chambers, where pillars and columns hold up walls full of stories. Ghosts? My stomach twinged. If Roald Dahl were here, he would have made the spooks spook. Humour is often the best form of defence. I shouted out loud: 'Bullshit'. The faces in the cliff called back '... shit ... shit ... shit'. Practice makes perfect, repetition brings strength and strength brings confidence. Louder, this time: 'Spooks, my arse'. The City Hall Caves encored back '... arse, arse, arse'. I swung my torch beam round, making walls move and columns dance. Confidence can also vanish in a flash. A voice from behind said, 'Good evening'. I spun round to a dark shape against the night. It asked, 'What are you photographing?' When humour fails, try attack for defence. 'The mayor's balls', I said. The torch caught a smile on his face, and then his laughter rang out from the dark. The City Hall Caves echoed 'ha-ha-ha'.

Can the haphazard become the orderly? Can less say more? How can contradiction bring harmony and confusion clarify? The painter adds and the photographer subtracts. My head is a reflection and sits with the gannets. How can quite dark look rather light? Thousands of seabirds screech, but the print is so quiet. The eye struggles to record movement, the camera not. Look at the birds – some are blurred. The setting was cold, but the torch added warmth. The gannets shit, we can't smell. I light the birds, and the rocks, my head and my feet. The torch disappears. On the horizon, a fishing boat moves across two planes of glass. The camera faces backwards, but actually records forwards. The picture is mute – but a foghorn sounds and pebbles crunch. One plus one shouldn't always be two. Hitch on the wings of a gannet, and fly.

Condoms for boys
eerie rooms of sand
clouds over solitaire
past wild horses on
long roads to Lüderitz

After years of vagabonding through southern Africa, you come to realise a couple of things. One is that you can't please all the people all the time. If you do, you'll be labelled a boring old fart. So as the kilometres, the mountains and the valleys, the deserts, and the years tick by, I've come to please fewer people some of the time, and only a couple of them most of the time. The sand dunes at Sossusvlei in the Namib Naukluft National Park are world-famous. They have been photographed, filmed, sketched and painted from every angle, corner, viewpoint and perspective imaginable. You know – cracked mud with sand dune, gemsbok with sand dune, tourists with sand dune, old acacia thorn tree with sand dune, thousands of times – by most of the people all the time. For this image, I wrote in my journal, 'The Namib monster must have died during the night. It had slid away down a dune and its tortured head looked sadly at the endless blue sky. Pentax 67, fisheye lens, 1/60 sec at f22.' Christiane Gehner is a world-famous picture editor and hates fisheye lenses. So this picture is for her, and all the conservationists, tourists, artists, wildlife fundis and boring old farts. Oh ... and the Toms and the Dicks, and the Harrys and the Janes. I hope nobody likes this photograph most of the time.

Dead tree and moon somewhere near Karasburg, Southern Namibia, '99.

View from Kuiseb Canyon Pass. Near the Namib Naukluft Park. Namibia. '99.

Cape Cross Seal Reserve. Skeleton Coast. Namibia. '97.

Farm labourers Markus and Koenap. Hammerstein Rest Camp. Namibia. '97.

School playground in evening light. Swakopmund. Namibia. '99.

Translated from German, 'Grasplatz' means 'Grass Place'. I sat on my camera case and surveyed the scene around me. There was a house on a hill and a sign next to a rusty railway track. The last train had passed there many years before, so nothing was going anywhere, and everything was doing absolutely nothing. I pushed my feet into the sand: the warmth from the day's heat gripped my toes. A big black ant, deciding it was time to move out of the desert, started crawling up my leg. It crawled upwards in such a pompous *windgat* [smart arse] manner that I wanted to smash the living shit out of it, but after glancing up at the deep blue sky, where God lives, I didn't. That's only because He said that we should love all creatures big and small. When the ant reached my knee, I spoke to it instead of smashing it. 'Do you know why this wasted, forlorn place, without a blade of grass in sight, should be called Grasplatz?' (The reader should be aware of the fact that I wanted to say 'godforsaken', but God was watching me, and checking on whether I was going to secretly smash the ant. Anyway, God's department that patrols this part of the earth also gets pretty bored, for here everything is doing absolutely nothing.) It was easy having a conversation with an ant because it moved its head from side to side and up and down, continually agreeing and disagreeing. I spoke again: 'Because, earlier this century, before the railroad, oxwagons that crossed the desert to Lüderitz left supplies, water and grass fodder here, to collect on their return journey'. It was getting pretty dark now, so I lit the surroundings with my torch. 'During the '60s, a Mr Stauch, the weight inspector, lived in the house on the hill. One of his duties was to keep the tracks free of sand and, probably, kill irritating things like you'. I flicked the ant off my leg into the 'Grasplatz' night.

Abandoned Grasplatz railway station. Namib Desert. Outside Lüderitz. Namibia. '97.

Wild horses of the Namib. Near Aus. Namib Naukluft National Park. Namibia. '97.

Late afternoon light on sand dunes outside Swakopmund. Namibia. '99.

The coastline north-west of Grosse Bucht is rugged and wild. Like troops into battle, the Namib pushed its rocks forward to fight. Yet the Atlantic enemy was great, bringing in waves, relentlessly. Great masses of water rolled in onto the land, attacking like a frenzied animal every piece of land. Like mortally injured soldiers, seaweed tentacles would roll back and forth, amongst the battle's froth. The smells are pungent and deadly sad. Rotten discarded kelp, broken seabirds and many tortured bloated seals. Massive banks of tired brown foam rise and fall, as if hiding a monster that refuses to die.

15° 5' East
26° 38' South

165

Bridge to Diaz Cross. Atlantic coastline near Lüderitz. Namibia. '99.

Looking North-West towards the Swakop River basin and Goanikontes oasis. Namibia. '99.

You approach Lüderitz from the east. From a long way off you can see the church, the water tanks and the houses clutching hold of the bare rock hills around the bay. The village always seems so forlorn, so lost in this vast landscape of desert. This place that lay ahead always brought with it some strangeness, as if time ticked slower and all things took longer. I reached down and fumbled amongst the collected rubbish on the car floor. It's difficult finding something whilst driving with one eye. The other one had to watch for sand dunes on the road. I pulled over, bowed my head on the steering wheel and smiled. Then I scribbled in my book: 'Freedom is driving, looking, scratching through shit you've collected since Chimanimani, with one eye, and watching out for sand dunes on the road with the other'. Usually, freedom is not finding what you're looking for, but this time I did. Then I drove on whilst Bob sang a song, 'How many roads must a man walk down before he can call himself a man? ... the answer my friend is blowing in the wind, the answer is blowing in the wind'. Just outside town I stopped again. The toilet was still there – all alone in the desert, blowing in the wind.

Toilet in the Namib Desert. Outside Lüderitz. Namibia. '99.

Road C13 from Helmeringhausen to Aus. Namibia. '99.

This is the story of horses, whisky and men. Also Road C13 going south-west to Aus, a small village on the edge of the Namib. Many years ago I travelled off this road, into the desert, happy-go-lucky, mindless and mad. Memories made in the desert remain lonely and stark. Somewhere near nowhere, the growl of the engine stopped and died in a squeak. Without the C13, I started to walk, south-west to Aus, happy-go-lucky, but mad. I walked till the hours turned and passed, going somewhere to nowhere. My head boiled, my throat thickened and my tongue dried out. Crack a joke, I said, humour yourself, I thought – ha-ha-ha. Death should be fun – tra-la-la. The sun started to hang low in the west. Then, finally, through the last shimmers of heat and dust and near-death, I came to Aus. It wasn't a mirage, because I touched a sign that said 'Aus'. Slowly, I walked up the main street alone, bowlegged like a cowboy – not from the toughness but from the chafing. They were real, the steps to the bar, and the old swing doors opened and closed in sad squeaks. The barman looked up, a little confused. I dusted myself, straightened my leather waistcoat and screwed up my eyes. Then I slammed my fist down on the counter and said, 'More whisky and fresh horses for my men!' An old man in the far corner shook his head, got up and left. Squeak-squeak. The barman looked dazed, scared, but managed to stutter, 'Sorry Mm ... Mi ... ster, what?' Down with the fist again: 'You heard me: more whisky and fresh horses for my men'. The barman paled, took fright, and ran out the bar. Squeak-squeak-squeak. I leant over the counter and took a beer. It's a long way through the desert to Aus.

169

Sometimes a man needs a shot – a shot of this, a shot of that, a shot of whisky, a shot in the dark, a photographic shot. There's nothing wrong with a shot or two. Just beware of too many shots. Photographically, one can *make* shots or one can *take* shots. You drive past the 'Happy Crab Snack Bar', and decide on a shot. A good shot can take a while to shoot. Finally, Beauty Mbangiswana comes out of the Happy Crab and you ask her if you can shoot her. After a bit of this and a bit of that, she leans on the pole and you take a shot. Two dudes want to join the shot. Then you have to up your act, and tell them you only do a shot at a time. Beauty is now starting to get restless, and you know very well that your first shot was a shit shot. You are skating on thin ice, even though you're hot and on the Namib's edge. You throw in your last shot: 'Beauty, my name is Obie and I collect condoms for my two sons. Does the Happy Crab have condoms? You know, coloured ones, like they have in South Africa? Those with the flag on them so the boys can feel they're *doing it* for their country. It would be nice taking some Namibian ones along, so they can get some international shots.' Beauty laughs. Lucky shot.

SOUTH AFRICAN
CONDOM

NAMIBIAN
CONDOM

I'll just be frank and say that Africa is rather a stuff-up. But then so am I, that's why I love it so much. I just hope that the African Renaissance changes some of that, but not all of it. What would people like me do then? This scene is also a self-portrait – a little colourful but transparent. What? Oh sorry, I am the vague reflection above the sand dune, to the left of the toilets and the bar. Sounds spot on. I have been here often before (not the café, but the bar). Such disappointment. ('Disappointed', as explained in the Tundura Factor 3, says that in Africa, disappointment is to know where you're going, but not to find what you're looking for.) I peered through glass and sighed: 'No weiswurst, no prätzels, no coffee, no beer, no schnapps. What a stuff-up, no nothing'. Then I became all enthusiastic and added a drop to the ocean and a grain to the sand dunes. Help the African Renaissance – make something out of nothing.

Christoph Lazarus and Petrus Igoga in front of the Bay View Hotel. Lüderitz. Namibia. '97.

Namibia was a German protectorate from 1884 to 1915. In Lüderitz, as in most other towns, German is still spoken by some of the older people. It was another sunny morning, just like most other mornings. The Bay View Hotel had very little view of the bay, yet its façade dazzled me with brightness. Mr Christoph Lazarus (holding crates) was being visually organised to enhance the rather adorned gables. Mr Petrus Igoga was holding the mop to illustrate the level of the road, and more important, to complement the big blob of red. Both Mr Lazarus and Mr Igoga were not over-friendly. This didn't really matter, as I'd paid them a large amount of money to be organised and, besides, this wasn't going to be a friendly picture. I was startled when a voice in German asked, 'Was fotografieren Sie, eigentlich?' He was a tourist, young, and wore sandals and socks. I can't be serious with anybody wearing sandals and socks. 'I am testing new emulsions for Agfa in the brightest spot on earth, investigating the high reflective index of the white façade, and the resulting absorption and luminosity on blue and red.' Said the sandals and socks, 'Ach so, danke schön.' A white bakkie passed the Bay Hotel.

Frederika Stoffel and friends. Township behind Lüderitz. Southern Namibia. '97.

A **photograph** is said to be worth a thousand words. This one has only 157 of them. Even that's too many. If you like only the pretty and good, page on. This image is titled 'Man urinating'. Often photographs deceive us, lull us with niceties and change reality. In Africa, we all live in the Happysadland. This photograph shows the Happy and cloaks the Sad. OK, it's obvious. The shacks – or better said, the informal settlement in the foreground – look quaint and colourful, but are really sad and not glad. No amenities, only hunger and crime. So most of us will sigh, shrug our shoulders and look beyond. How idyllic: anchored boats and lapping waters. Back to reality: along the bay there's a sign that reads, 'Beware, do not eat any shellfish'. [Why? High levels of *E. coli* present in the seawater.] All around my camera's position were rocky hills with thousands of human faeces. It was a minefield. Conclusion: this photograph is worth a thousand turds.

Frederika Stoffel and friends. Township behind Lüderitz. Southern Namibia. '97.

*T*he **authorities** from Namdeb Diamond Mines gave me permission to work in Kolmanskop after sunset. How enthralling a situation, roaming around a ghost town after dark. The hospital was a long building and was set some way back from the main complex. Since the village was abandoned in about 1911, the Namib Desert has pushed sand against the outer walls. I sat a long while on my camera case, quite still, peering down the long passage. What a phenomenon this Namib was: like a slow and timeless great beast, it had pushed its sands through the windows, the doors, into every crevice and crack. The sun had long set, but the surrounding desert seemed to hold the light, push it up to heaven, reflect it back into the dark rooms with forgotten stories. In places of great quietude, human thoughts become motionless, yet this stillness can amplify emotions, free unlocked spirits. No, not spooks and ghosts and funny transparent things. Eerie had a smell, an old aroma of diamond stories mixed with sand. Eerie was here, all around, down the passage and in every ward.

At Sossusvlei you get some of the highest sand dunes in the world. Sometimes, when the sparse rains fall in the Namib, the *vleie*, or depressions, beneath the sand dunes fill with water. Later, the mud dries and cracks, turning the *vlei* into a large hard pan. On this day there were many tourists around. Germans wearing sandals and socks, French clutching Perrier water bottles, and South Africans looking for places to braai. They were all photographing each other standing in front of the dunes. Hans with Gertrude, Pierre holding Brigitte, then Piet, Jan and Sannie. Oh, sorry, under the giant acacia tree sat Tom, Dick and Hassan, two of them very dazed and pink – probably 'Poms'. Bent over like a tracking Bushman, I followed a set of footprints across the pan. A while later, Dick with the white legs and the red neck strolled over and asked, 'Excuse me, why *that* one?' 'Well,' I answered, throwing in a long pause, 'when it rains in the Namib, the Bushmen migrate ... mmm ... from the Kalahari Desert, following the age-old tradition. Ja, the ancient Mud Race. All young male Bushmen run across the ... mmm ... moor. The last one to lose the last bit of mud between his toes gets to take the prettiest maiden across the dunes.'

The dust road stretches in front of the traveller's eye. The road is like a long elongated triangle of vibrating tyre marks, which pull broadly across the windscreen, then bounce and jumble and zigzag to a distant spot – the vagabond's vanishing point. A point that eludes, defies, yet nourishes the traveller's heart. For him, the first horizon is just the harbinger of another one, and freedom lies on the road that slowly changes everything and all. A road that is alive, that dominates you and shakes you, and humbles you and the soul who holds the wheel. 'Corrugations, corrugations, why so long? Corrugations, corrugations becomes a song'. Perhaps freedom means watching a star at night and chasing a vanishing point at day. Then one fine restless day, at twilight time, you'll stop a while to rest. How can a place with so little give so much? Without a doubt, happiness is to look so far, around and around, then to hug your car at Solitaire.

View of the manager's house and Scottie the dog. Kolmanskop. Near Lüderitz. Namibia. '97.